DEVOTIONAL WARM-UPS

for the

CHURCH CHOIR

DEDICATION

To the many choir members that I have had the privilege of leading during these past 35 years in seven churches in the Grand Rapids area.

DEVOTIONAL WARM-UPS

for the

CHURCH CHOIR

Weekly devotional lessons and discussions
for choir members to provide training
in leadership and worship.

by
Kenneth W. Osbeck
Assisted by David C. Egner
Foreword by C. Harry Causey

KREGEL PUBLICATIONS
Grand Rapids, Michigan 49501

Library of Congress Cataloging-in-Publication Data

Osbeck, Kenneth W.
  Devotional Warm-ups for the Church Choir

    1. Choirs (Music)—Prayer-books and devotions—
English. I. Title.
BV4596.C48072   1985   242'.68   85 -17222
ISBN 0-8254-3421-1 (pbk.)

First printing 1985
Reprinted 1986

Printed in the United States of America

CONTENTS

FOREWORD

The pastor of one of the largest churches in the world rises early and spends several consecutive hours in prayer each day! Those who know his demanding schedule and massive responsibilities are amazed. They ask, "How can you afford so much time in prayer?" His response is always calmly consistent: "I can't afford not to!"

No choir, which is *called to lead* in the *worship* of our Lord Jesus Christ, can afford not to spend some of its precious preparation time in focusing on Him. The worship choir has one primary purpose, and that is to minister to the Lord. Oh, that every director and choir member would fully understand the absolute necessity of those quality moments in that rehearsal spent with the Father. Our spiritual preparation is really more vital than our musical preparation!

Ken Osbeck is qualified to bring these spiritual pearls, for his own heart, mind and spirit are dedicated to the Lordship of Christ. His approach is to teach us, equip us, inspire us, and then move us to involvement with one another as he follows each devotional with a stimulating and sobering discussion question.

Your choir will grow through the use of *Devotional Warm-ups*...They will grow close to their Lord, they will grow in depth of understanding of their true ministry, and they will grow closer to one another. And when these growth points are truly evident, I would not be surprised to see them also grow in numbers!

So I encourage you to allow God's Holy Spirit to work through the ministry of Ken Osbeck, allowing your choir to be all that God wants it to be. And don't be surprised when these warm-ups cause your choir to sing better!

C. Harry Causey

President and Editor, MUSIC REVELATION
Conductor, The National Christian Choir

PREFACE

This booklet is written to provide weekly inspirational and instructional material for use in church choir rehearsals. Its primary purpose is to help choir members focus their attention upon God and to strengthen their music ministry. Choirs that conduct their rehearsal during the midweek service will find this booklet ideal for their own devotional times. It will serve well as a basis for helpful discussion in these sessions.

Choir rehearsal time is usually far too short to accomplish musically all that any director desires to achieve. Even so, time should be set aside for the development of the spiritual content found in this booklet. The devotional warm-ups can be used in a variety of ways, depending upon the needs of the choir and the time allotted. The choir experience should include a time and place for individual spiritual growth and fellowship. Because in a sense a choir is a church within a church, the members should be encouraged to share their joys and prayer concerns as an integral part of each rehearsal.

The general topics covered are spread over a proposed, ten-month choir season with four devotional discussions each month. Three additional topics are provided for those months having five rehearsals.

Christian leaders and choir members also need to develop a greater understanding and deeper appreciation of the important days and seasons throughout the church year. Included in these devotional studies are discussions for such days and seasons as:

Reformation Day, All Saints Day, Advent Season, Christmas, Epiphany, Lent, Easter, Pentecost, the Christian home, and patriotic days.

Our prayer is that God will use these devotional warm-ups to help you grow spiritually, to strengthen your choir ministry, and to bring rich blessing to your congregation and community.

INTRODUCTION

While I was working recently on an up-dated edition of the *Pocket Guide for the Church Choir Member* with the book editor of Kregel Publications, Paul W. Bennehoff, he remarked: "But, Ken, don't choir members also have to be prepared spiritually as well as musically? Don't we need a complementary booklet for choirs that would give more emphasis and training to the biblical and spiritual implications of the church music ministry? Don't choir members as well as the pastor and director need training to lead others in worship?" The more we talked, the more enthused we both became about such a project. I began to realize anew the unusual potential that exists in an adult choir. If each member became better informed and more earnestly concerned about relating his/her musical ministry to the furtherance of the Christian message as a committed leader for God, much could be accomplished for His glory.

I shared these thoughts with David Egner, writer and editor with the Radio Bible Class and contributor to *Our Daily Bread.* Together we developed a growing awareness that the church choir should be one of the key influences in the spiritual dynamic of any local church. We also realized that choir members must not only be trained musically and spiritually for public leadership, but that the choir experience itself represents opportunities for unusual spiritual growth and Christian fellowship for the individual member.

The earnest prayer of each of us is that this devotional booklet will stimulate church choir members to appreciate anew the importance of their local church and the role of the choir in providing inspiring leadership in the services. May they also realize that individual living must always model the reality of the truths proclaimed in one's public ministries.

***

O God of eternal beauty and harmony, Who has ordained
that men shall declare Your glory in the joy of music,
Anoint with Your Spirit all who, by voice or instrument,
lead the praises of Your people,
That in sincerity and truth, we may ever magnify Your
name in concert with saints and angels. Amen.

THE MARVEL OF THE HUMAN VOICE
Respect and Concern

My lips will shout for joy when I sing praise to You (Psalm 71:23).

The voice is one of God's choicest gifts to man. It gives us the ability to communicate our thoughts and feelings vocally. One of the important arguments in support of creationism—that man is the image bearer of God and not the result of mere chance evolution—is that only man has been given the ability to communicate an organized language with a voice. Even more, we can enhance our verbal and emotional expressions with musical sounds of pitch, duration, harmonies—WE CAN SING!

The psalmist exclaimed: "I praise You because I am fearfully and wonderfully made" (Psa. 139:14). Part of the awe-inspiring and marvelous make-up of our bodies is the voice. We do not need to understand all of the scientific intricacies of our vocal mechanism to appreciate the wonder of communication. One of life's most difficult burdens is simply the loss of the human voice.

"It is good to sing praises to our God; for it is pleasant, and praise is comely" [proper] (Psa. 147:1). There is a personal therapeutic value for the individual who learns to enjoy the activity of singing. It is also an activity that pleases God. Because singing is normal human behavior, almost without exception everyone can learn to sing. The voice, researchers tell us, is one of the best reflections of the personality, for it reveals the real "you" of any person. It follows, then, that developing oneself as an individual should improve the voice—and, in turn, that improving the voice should make a better person.

The choir member should learn to treat his voice with respect and to take proper care of this choice instrument. To sing well on Sunday requires not only musical and spiritual preparation, but also adequate rest on Saturday night. A singer must be careful not to strain the voice with overuse before the Sunday services. It is also important to eat and drink properly prior to singing. If hoarseness and laryngitis persist, one should seek professional medical advice.

Above all, a choir member needs to be in tune with God with his mind and heart, so that the voice will reflect the genuineness of his personal relationship with the Creator.

Come, we that love the Lord, and let our joys be known.
Join in a song with sweet accord and thus surround the throne.   —Isaac Watts

GROUP DISCUSSION
In what ways can our voices reflect our physical, emotional and spiritual condition? If our individual hearts and voices are not singing, what might this possibly say about our total view of life? If this congregation does not sing well, what can this reflect about our church life?

SUGGESTED GROUP SINGING
Joyful, Joyful, We Adore Thee, No. 51—*101 Hymn Stories*
In My Heart There Rings a Melody, No. 45—*101 More Hymn Stories*

THOUGHT
The voice you are born with is God's gift to you; the use of your voice is your gift to God.

O God of creation, thank You for the gift of my voice. Thank You for the opportunity to use it for Your glory during this new choir season. Together may our voices and our lives blend well that we may offer You the praise You deserve. May the sounds of our voices be pleasing to You. We pray this in Your Son's holy name. Amen.

THE MARVEL OF THE HUMAN VOICE
Instrument of Highest Praise

Let everything that hath breath praise the Lord (Psalm 149:1; 150:3-6).

The human voice is not only a choice gift of God to man; it is in turn an instrument of sublime worth for man to use in offering praise to the Almighty. Through song we can express our loftiest thoughts about God and His creation. Not all of us may be able to sing tunefully, but when opportunities are presented, everyone in whom the Spirit of God dwells can and should respond with joyful praise.

The human voice is the most perfect of all musical instruments. We never cease to thrill at hearing the rich resonance of a low voice or the lilting, soaring beauty of a lovely tenor or soprano. All man-made musical instruments are mere imitations of the human voice. The psalmist declared, "I will sing of the love of the Lord forever; with my mouth will I make Your faithfulness known through all generations" (Psa. 89:1). God is glorified when our voices are raised in praise of Him. "Whoso offereth praise glorifieth Me" (Psa. 50:23).

Praise is the predominant theme of the Scriptures. The first reference to music in the Bible is found in Genesis 4:24: "His brother's name was Jubal; he was the father of all who play the harp and flute." The musician's roots, then, can be traced away back to Jubal, who is mentioned in concert with the one who first raised food (Jabal) and the one who first fabricated tools for industrial use (Tubal-Cain). Thus, from the very beginning days of mankind, God made provision for the aesthetic—the soul expressions of man through music.

Furthermore, all important interventions of God with mankind are accompanied by some form of praise: creation (Job 38:7), the incarnation (Luke 2:8-14), our personal salvation experience (Luke 15:7), Christ's return (1 Cor. 15:52), His eternal

12

reign (Rev. 19:6-8). Even as God accompanies, with music, all of His encounters with man, we, as redeemed people, have the privilege of worshiping Him with voices of praise now and of preparing for our prime occupation throughout eternity. Until that day, may we know in part the joy of glorifying God, as we join our voices in praise of Him, who died that we might live to sing eternally.

Praise the Savior, ye who know Him! Who can tell how much we owe Him?

Gladly let us render to Him all we are and have.

—Thomas Kelly

GROUP DISCUSSION

Why is a believer's "praise life" so important to his own general well-being? How can our "praise life" be improved both individually and corporately? In what ways besides singing can we offer praise to the Lord? How can the praise of God through singing be called a part of God's eternal praise?

SUGGESTED GROUP SINGING

O For a Thousand Tongues, No. 65—*101 Hymn Stories*
Sing Praise to God Who Reigns Above, No. 81—*101 Hymn Stories*

THOUGHT

He who sincerely praises God will soon discover within his soul an inclination to praise goodness in his fellow men.

THE MARVEL OF THE HUMAN VOICE
Instrument of Healing

In the night His song shall be with me (Psalm 42:8).

Most believers have at some time experienced the healing power of sacred music. They have come to a church service with their hearts filled with fear and anxiety or their spirits drooping with an onslaught of depression. Some have been forced to go through unusual physical, financial, or emotional difficulties throughout the past week. The daily demands of living have produced a mountain of despondency. But then is heard a triumphant anthem of praise, a majestic hymn of worship, or a simple gospel song that reminds them of God's nearness and guidance. The struggling Christian's burden is lifted, his mind becomes clear, his fragile emotions are mended, and his heart once again is able to sing, as he returns to his busy world of activity.

In this way the voice becomes an instrument of healing. Life's deepest emotions—joy, love, sorrow—are often best expressed with a song (Isa. 30:29; Job 30:31). Therefore, choir members are called to be ministers, not performer-entertainers. They are to care for the spiritual and emotional needs of God's people through the vehicle of music—to provide songs of comfort and encouragement for the night seasons of life. The verb "minister" is derived from the Hebrew word that means "to share." The choir member is, therefore, involved in a humble yet exalted service associated with the spiritual activities of ministering. He is directing needy and often hurting lives to the One who is the ultimate source of all true comfort and contentment. In the service of God there is no place for a "super star." The calling for each of us is simply that of a humble servant—a reflector of the Son! "And whosoever will be chief among you, let him be your servant: even as the Son of man came not to be ministered unto, but to minister" (Matt. 20:27, 28).

As we minister God's healing to others through music, our own emotions will be purged and our hearts will be lifted. We feel refreshed after a service of worship in which we have truly ministered. There is a personal therapy, not only for those who hear, but also for those who minister spiritually with sacred song.

May we always be sensitive to the needs of others and willing to share comfort and encouragement, even as troubled Saul was restored through the healing music of the psalmist David (1 Sam. 16).

Come, ye disconsolate, where'er ye languish—
Come to the mercy seat, fervently kneel;
Here bring your wounded hearts, here tell your anguish:
Earth has no sorrow that heav'n cannot heal.

—Thomas Moore and Thomas Hastings

GROUP DISCUSSION

Share an experience of when a song was especially helpful to you spiritually. When we sing, how can we feel more strongly and empathize more fully with the cares, joys and concerns of this congregation?

SUGGESTED GROUP SINGING

From Every Stormy Wind That Blows, No. 24—*101 Hymn Stories*

Near to the Heart of God, No. 63—*101 More Hymn Stories*

THOUGHT

Satan fears music as much as the strong preaching of the Word, since music drives the devil away and makes people happy.

—Martin Luther

THE MARVEL OF THE HUMAN VOICE
Instrument of Witness

I will praise You, O Lord, among the peoples: I will sing to You among the nations (Psalm 57:9).

The music of the church should always be a compelling witness to the non-believer. Hymns of worship exalt God as Creator, Sustainer, and Redeemer. Anthems of praise tell the unsaved world what God is like. Songs of testimony are a means of telling the non-Christian about the happiness, peace, and forgiveness that come to those who place their trust in Christ. And joyous gospel songs personalize the truth that Christ died for them. One of the strongest impacts we believers can make upon an unbeliever attending our services is to make him aware of a congregation that is sincerely absorbed in worship and the proclamation of truth through sacred song. Too often the non-Christian sees merely a group of apathetic spectators waiting to be entertained.

In Muskegon, Michigan, there was a small neighborhood church where the pastor, saved from an early life of playing the trumpet for a jazz band in Chicago, appreciated in an unusual way the power of music to testify of Christ. His Sunday evening services were always characterized by enthusiastic, cheerful singing. In the summertime he would say, "Open the windows. We're not ashamed to have our neighbors hear about Christ." During the course of his ministry, several families began attending services and eventually became Christians, because they were attracted to the gospel through the witness of music.

As a choir, we should assume that there are unbelievers in every service. The songs we choose and the vitality with which we sing will be a witness to those who hear. If we view the congregation as merely an audience of spectators to be entertained, we will miss the unique opportunity before us to make an impact for Christ. As we sing, we must always see people as those for whom the Savior died, as individuals walking in darkness, who need to be directed to the One who alone is the Light of Life. And may the non-believers who are present see and hear an authentic gospel that is clearly demonstrated by those who claim to believe it.

> We've a song to be sung to the nations that shall lift their hearts to the Lord,
> A song that shall conquer evil and shatter the spear and sword. —H. Ernest Nichol

GROUP DISCUSSION

Share an instance when you knew that a sacred song was a witness in influencing a person's decision to become a Christian. In what ways can music be rightly used as a tool for witnessing? Is it possible to use music wrongly as an influence to reach the unsaved—for example, as a manipulator of the human emotions?

SUGGESTED GROUP SINGING

I Love to Tell the Story, No. 37—*101 Hymn Stories*
Room at the Cross for You, No. 74—*101 More Hymn Stories*

THOUGHT

Singing does at least as much as preaching to impress the Word of God upon people's minds. —Dwight L. Moody

Dear God, may our voices and our lives blend well as we praise You. Keep us from thinking of ourselves only as singer-performers. Help us rather to be witnesses for Christ and proclaimers of the good news. May we ever sing with sincerity and reality. Use our music this year, we pray, to be a clear witness to some unbelievers about Christ, in whose name we pray. Amen.

MUSIC AND THE OLD TESTAMENT
A Way of Life

Praise the Lord with the harp; make melody to Him (Psalm 33:2).

The pages of the Old Testament are alive with the sounds of music. In fact, Jewish history is synonymous with song. From the joyous songs of the Exodus onward, the deep religious feelings of the Jewish faithful were made known in song and dance. And no person contributed more to the role of music in Jewish life than King David, who is known as the "sweet singer of Israel." The entire book of 150 Psalms is believed to have been a book of Jewish worship and praise songs in their original form. In marked contrast to the contemporary pagan religions of that day, the Israelites were known for their exalted use of music in the worship of the one true God, Jehovah.

The joy of Jewish song was stilled temporarily during the Babylonian exile. One of the songs, Psalm 137, records their sad laments during that time. When the Jews returned to Jerusalem under the leadership of Zerubbabel, Ezra, and Nehemiah to rebuild the temple, happy singing returned. Music was always an important indicator of Israel's relationship with God. Whenever it was absent from the service of Jehovah, it marked a time of judgment and spiritual desolation.

Music was an integral part of Old Testament life. It was the natural expression of the lifestyle for the Israelites on every occasion, both secular and religious.

* *Religious*—worship for Israel found its richest expression in music (1 Chron. 15:14, 27, 28; 16:4-7, 23-30; 25:1-31; 2 Chron. 30:21; Neh. 12:45-47).

* *Social*—important social occasions such as weddings were made more significant through music (1 Sam. 18:6, 7; 1 Chron. 15:29; Jer. 7:34).

* *Funerals*—music used at times of mourning as well as times of gladness. Note the dirge (funeral song) sung by David

with the deaths of Saul and Jonathon (2 Sam. 1:18-27). It became customary to hire professional musicians to assist at funerals (Matt. 9:23).

Economic—important times related to the prosperity of the Jews, such as grape gatherings and grain harvests, were celebrated with music (Isa. 16:10; 27:2; Jer. 48:33).

Political—when a king was crowned, great sounds of music helped celebrate the coronations (1 Kings 1:39, 40; 2 Kings 9:13; 11:14; 2 Chron. 23:11-13). When military victories were celebrated, the people expressed their joy with voices and instruments (Ex. 15:1-21; Judg. 5:1-31; 11:34; 1 Sam. 18:6, 7; 2 Chron. 20:21, 22; 27, 28).

Yes, the Old Testament pages echo with the sound of music, a natural response for God's people in any age to express their deepest feelings of joy, gratitude and praise—A WAY OF LIFE!

GROUP DISCUSSION

Though it is important to sing in church, why is it even more important that a Christian carry his song into every area of life?

SUGGESTED GROUP SINGING

It Is Well With My Soul, No. 44—*101 Hymn Stories*
Satisfied, No. 75—*101 More Hymn Stories*

THOUGHT

Christianity is not a theory or speculation, but a life; not a philosophy of life, but a living presence. This realization can turn any gloom into a song.   —Samuel Taylor Coleridge

Dear Heavenly Father, help me to carry the music of this church into my daily living. May my life be characterized with Thy joy. Show me when my witness for You is weakened by a wrong attitude. And let the music of our choir challenge each believer with the goal of victorious, joyful living that will ever glorify You. In Jesus' name. Amen.

MUSIC AND THE OLD TESTAMENT
Misusing the Gift

Take away from Me the noise of thy songs, for I will not hear the melody of thine harps (Amos 5:23).

God Himself is the originator of music. He placed in man alone the ability to understand, develop and appreciate this unique gift. Man, therefore, has two choices: he can either use this gift for the glory of God and the ennoblement of his fellow-man, or he can exploit it for sensual gratification and the debasement of others.

Music has as much potential for evil as it has for good. The following words were used in Ezekiel 28:13 to describe Satan: "The workmanship of your timbrels and pipes was prepared for you on the day you were created." This means that Satan was originally created to be an angelic being of praise and adoration to God; he was a veritable musical instrument. But he turned all that potential for beauty inward and fell victim to his own pride and ambition. Perhaps this explains why many people are so easily enthralled by sensuous music or a fleshly expression of it. The result is that, rather than being a blessing to mankind, music often becomes a curse—"noise" that God refuses to hear!

The kind of music we select and the way we use it become, to those who hear our singing, a vital demonstration of our concept of God and of our spiritual integrity. These choices show our values and priorities and reveal to others our true selves.

Sad to say, the church choir has often been a place where music is misused. Often there are songs used that present a distorted or "cheap" gospel. Church musicians have sometimes demanded special treatment and have earned the label "trouble-makers." More than one church choir has been called "the war department." Musicians have even been the cause of church divisions and splits. Regardless of vocal ability, there is no place in a ministry for a prima-donna attitude. Any church choir will be much more effective with singers of average vocal abilities but dedicated hearts than with a full choir loft of mere worldly-minded professionals. The essence of singing for the worldly musician is self-expression and self-exploitation. The essence of the ministry, whether it is given through the spoken or sung word, must always be the exaltation of Christ, concern for others, and the crucifixion of self.

The Scriptures teach that our worship and praise must always be consistent with righteous living and social justice. Without this consistency, our praise becomes an abomination to the Lord—songs that He refuses to hear! May it never be necessary for God to say to this church choir or congregation as He did to the Israelites of old, "Take away from Me the noise of thy songs ..." (Amos 5:23).

"Take my voice and let me sing always, only, for my King."
—Frances R. Havergal

GROUP DISCUSSION

In what ways do you feel music can be misused in the local church? In what ways can music be misused in one's personal life? In the home? Can you suggest at least three criteria for choosing music for church use? For home listening?

SUGGESTED GROUP SINGING

Take My Life and Let It Be, No. 87—*101 Hymn Stories*
A Charge to Keep I Have, No. 1—*101 More Hymn Stories*

THOUGHT

Give me the making of the songs of a nation, and I care not who makes its laws.   —Andrew Fletcher (1665-1716)

Rules without a relationship lead to rebellion. Rules with a relationship lead to a loving response.

MUSIC IN THE OLD TESTAMENT
A Musical Overview

*Then sang Moses and the children of Israel this song. . .I will sing
unto the Lord,. . .the Lord is my strength and song, and He is become my salvation; He is my God. . .(Exodus 15:1, 2).*

Each choir member should realize with conviction that he or
she has a vital place in the great heritage of the Christian church.
Having their roots in Hebrew worship and continuing throughout church history, choirs have been an important factor in
corporate worship. The pages of the Old Testament reveal
much about singers, instrumentalists, and choir members.

*Individual Musicians. One of the earliest was Moses, who
led the people of Israel in singing of God's power and deliverance from the Egyptians (Ex. 15). Deborah and Barak are
recorded as lifting glad voices in praise to God for their miracu-
lous victory over the Canaanites (Judg. 5:1, 2). Asaph led a
group of instrumentalists and singers when the ark was brought
to Jerusalem (1 Chron. 15 and 16). Other musicians mentioned
include Jeduthum (1 Chron. 16:38, 42), Chenaniah (1 Chron.
15:27), and Habakkuk (Hab. 3:19).

*Organized Choirs. The Old Testament also tells about a
number of organized choirs. One of them is David's tabernacle
choir, composed of ten men and a director (1 Chron. 15:12-22).
King Solomon organized a 4,000-voice choir for the dedication
of the temple, and its awe-inspiring performance was accompanied by a large body of instruments which filled the house
with the glory of God (1 Chron. 23:5; 27-32; 2 Chron. 5:11-14).
Zerubbabel's temple choir was composed of 200 mixed voices
(Ezra 2:41, 65, 70). Nehemiah's choir had 245 voices (Neh. 7:1;
11:22, 23). Josephus, the noted first-century Jewish historian,
states that there had been as many as 200,000 individuals
trained for the musical portions of the temple service.

*Practices and Procedures. Evidently a special school was
established in Solomon's day for training musicians—288
people taught the singers in the temple choir (1 Chron. 25:7, 8).
The musicians were referred to as "seers," implying that they

had special spiritual insights (1 Chron. 25:5). Since the notation of music was not yet established, the music was learned by rote and likely sung in unison with instrumental accompaniment. Likely the melodies were chant-like with a limited compass in range and sung with much embellishment. The "selahs" are thought to have been instrumental interludes in order to give the singers and worshipers opportunity to reflect upon what they had sung.

Antiphonal singing was widely used in temple worship— different choirs and groups of instruments answering each other, or by the choir answering a leader. This was made possible by the rendition of the parallel couplets into which most Hebrew poetry is grouped, and which form a series of balancing phrases. For example, Psalm 24:

a. The earth is the Lord's, and the fulness thereof;

b. The world, and they that dwell therein. etc.

This antiphonal singing afterwards became a prominent feature of early Christian worship.

Though music had an exalted place in the worship and praise of Jehovah, the people of the congregation were basically passive. They were not actively involved in the worship because the leaders (Levites) offered the praise on behalf of the people. In the New Testament church active lay participation should be the goal of every service.

GROUP DISCUSSION

What practical lessons can we learn from the Old Testament about music and worship?

SUGGESTED GROUP SINGING

Guide Me, O Thou Great Jehovah, No. 26—*101 Hymn Stories*

THOUGHT

Where your pleasure is, there is your treasure. Where your treasure is, there is your heart. Where your heart is, there is your happiness.   —Augustine

MUSIC AND THE OLD TESTAMENT
Requirements of Leaders

Then David spoke to the leaders of the Levites to appoint their brethren to be the singers accompanied by instruments of music, stringed instruments, harps, and cymbals, by raising the voice with resounding joy (1 Chronicles 15:16).

The Levites, members of one of the twelve tribes, were the appointed music leaders of the Old Testament. They were recognized as performing an important and sacred function in Israelite worship. They had to meet certain strict requirements and qualifications, because they were in the service of a holy God. Consider ten of these conditions, recorded in the Old Testament. They were to be

1. *Especially chosen from the Levitical priesthood*—not just anyone could serve in this capacity (1 Chron. 15:1, 2; 11-22; 16:4-7; 37:41, 42; 2 Chron. 20:21; Neh. 7:1).

2. *Well organized*—they were assigned specific work and were individually appointed to their tasks (2 Chron. 7:6; 8:14; 31:2; Neh. 11:2).

3. *Educated and trained*—teachers as well as scholars (1 Chron. 15:22; 25:1-8; Neh. 11:22; 12:42, 46).

4. *Efficient performers*—punctual and systematic. Note that the word "skillful" is used of them often (1 Chron. 16:37; 2 Chron. 8:14; 15:22; 31:2).

5. *Consecrated:* that is, they were to have clean hands and pure hearts (Num. 8:5-16; 1 Chron. 15:12, 14, 16; 2 Chron. 5:11, 12).

6. *Models of obedience to God's Word* (2 Chron. 34:30-32).

7. *Set apart by wearing distinctive robes* (1 Chron. 15:27; 2 Chron. 5:12).

8. *Recognized and paid for their services* (Num. 18:21; 2 Chron. 31:2-10; Neh. 12:47; 13:5, 10, 11). Homes were

24

to be provided for them as well (Ezra 2:70; Neh. 7:73; 12:28, 29).

9. *Treated as other religious leaders,* with no discrimination (Ezra 7:24; Neh. 10:28, 29, 39).

10. *Mature* (only those aged thirty and over). This was not a service to be performed by the young and inexperienced (Num. 4:47; 1 Chron. 23:3-5).

To minister musically in the Old Testament times was a great privilege and a most responsible service. It required choice people who were well prepared. This is still true of a church music-ministry today. In a very real sense we are New Testament Levites. Therefore, these principles established by God for the Levitical priesthood should be noted as valid guidelines for music leaders in a New Testament church.

Immortal, invisible, God only wise,
In light inaccessible hid from our eyes,
Most blessed, most glorious, the Ancient of Days,
Almighty, victorious—Thy great name we praise.
—Walter Chalmers Smith

GROUP DISCUSSION
In what ways are the above requirements and conditions for Levitical leadership in the Old Testament applicable to our music leadership in the local church today? Should persons with excellent voices be allowed to sing in a church service even if their lifestyle and Christian testimony are questionable?

SUGGESTED GROUP SINGING
Am I a Soldier of the Cross? No. 6—*101 More Hymn Stories*
Jesus, I My Cross Have Taken, No. 49—*101 More Hymn Stories*

THOUGHT
The Christian life that is joyless is a discredit to God and a disgrace to itself.   —Maltbie D. Babcock

PEOPLE OF PRAISE AND THANKSGIVING
For Our Heritage—All Saints Day

Wherefore seeing we also are compassed about with so great a cloud of witnesses. . .and let us run with patience the race that is set before us (Hebrews 12:1).

Throughout both the Old and New Testament times, God's people have been called to be people of praise and thanksgiving in order to represent the character and worth of the Almighty. Such a calling implies that God's people are to be living demonstrations to a defiled world of a victorious, joyful lifestyle.

As God's ambassador-representatives, our attitude toward life is one of the most important factors in our witness and ministry. Our life of praise should include sincere thanksgiving for our Christian heritage, for our daily, present blessings, and for the anticipation of our future inheritance—an eternal heaven.

One of the neglected days in many Protestant churches is All Saints Day, the first Sunday in November. This neglect is understandable, because the tradition of the day is rooted in medieval Catholicism. Homage is given on this day to the departed, canonized saints of the church.

There is, however, underlying meaning to this day that evangelical Protestants should use and recognize:

* *Every believer is called to be a saint* here and now. (Note the apostle Paul's addresses to Christians in his various epistles in the New Testament).

* *We are "surrounded by a cloud of witnesses"*—(parents, family, faithful pastors, teachers and friends)—who have or are contributing much to our lives.

* *Reminders of the memories* of those believers from this local fellowship who were called to their heavenly home during the past year.

For many of us, one particular individual has especially influenced our lives—directing us to God, tutoring us in truth, and modeling the virtues of the Christian life. For me, that person was my father, Emil Osbeck. Though he had only an eighth grade education, Dad used his life to represent God both in daily living and in his church ministry. As a painter-decorator for many years, he became known to his many customers as "the singing painter." Singing his favorite hymns while he worked became his natural way of life. At his funeral, many of his customers told me of the impact my father had upon their lives as they observed his cheerful attitude while working. One of his favorite Sunday afternoon activities was visiting nursing homes, where he would move from one bedside to another with words and songs of cheer. Though the name of Emil Osbeck will never appear in the annals of church history, in my memory he is one of God's choicest saints.

For all the saints who from their labors rest, who Thee by
faith before the world confessed,
Thy name, O Jesus, be forever blest. Alleluia!

—William W. How

GROUP DISCUSSION
Share the memory of some individual who especially influenced your life for God. Recall and share remembrances of individuals from this church and perhaps the choir who have left lasting memories and for which we can give thanks today.

SUGGESTED GROUP SINGING
For All the Saints, No. 25—*101 More Hymn Stories*
Living for Jesus, No. 56—*101 More Hymn Stories*

THOUGHT
Saints are persons who make it easier for others to believe in God.

O Almighty Lord, help us to honor You in our daily living. May we always cherish the memory of those who have contributed spiritual meaning to our lives. Give us a greater desire to be a tutor and model to others. **Amen.**

PEOPLE OF PRAISE AND THANKSGIVING
For Our Present Blessings

Bless the Lord, O my soul; and all that is within me, bless His holy name.

Bless the Lord, O my soul; and forget not all His benefits (Psalm 103:1, 2).

One important plateau of Christian maturity is learning to enjoy our personal relationship with God and to appreciate and be content with the benefits He provides. Too often believers give the impression that the Christian experience is a joyless journey consisting of harsh rules and regulations that must be painfully endured, until the heavenly rewards are finally realized. No joy or praise is evident in their Christian experience.

Praise and thanksgiving could be described in a general sense as a response of personal gratitude for the goodness and blessings of God—a heartfelt "thank you" from a redeemed creature for the daily benefits provided by the divine Creator. We pray often that God will bless us. Such praying is self-motivated. Scripture teaches that our prayers should include our blessing the Lord and remembering His many benefits. Consider these "benefits" listed in Psalm 103:

Forgives all our inquities, heals our diseases, redeems our life from destruction, crowns us with lovingkindness and mercy, satisfies us with good things, renews our youth, works righteousness and judgment for the oppressed, gives guidance to His people, is merciful, is gracious and slow to anger while plenteous in mercy, knows all about us, will never forsake.

In the Old Testament period, Levitical priests offered blood sacrifices to God on behalf of their people. In this New Testament era, believer-priests are also required to make offerings— the spiritual sacrifice of themselves:

I beseech you therefore, brethren, by the mercies of God, that you present your bodies a living sacrifice, holy, acceptable unto God, which is your reasonable service (Romans 12:1).

Other important spiritual sacrifices desired by God from each believer-priest are:

PRAISE, THANKSGIVING, GOOD WORKS, and COMMUNICATING

By Him therefore let us offer the sacrifice of praise to God continually, that is, the fruit of our lips giving thanks to His name. But to do good and to communicate forget not: for with such sacrifices God is well pleased (Hebrews 13:15, 16).

Have you ever considered your voice as one of the spiritual sacrifices that please God? This gift-offering carries with it the most personal reflection of His presence in our lives.

As God's people, let us offer the sacrifice of praise to the One from whom all blessings flow. May praise and thanksgiving be our daily antidotes for overcoming those blue moods of depression and self-pity that so easily beset each of us. May our times of corporate worship be acceptable to God because they come from thankful, praising hearts.

Praise God from whom all blessings flow; Praise Him, all creatures here below;

Praise Him above, ye heav'nly host; Praise Father, Son, and Holy Ghost.   —Thomas Ken

GROUP DISCUSSION

Share an experience in which you recall consciously changing a blue mood of depression or self-pity into a happy occasion by offering to God a sacrifice of praise and thanksgiving.

SUGGESTED GROUP SINGING

Count Your Blessings, No. 16—*101 Hymn Stories*
Thanks to God!, No. 85—*101 More Hymn Stories*

THOUGHT

Praise not only frees us; it directs us to a Source that is greater than ourselves.

PEOPLE OF PRAISE AND THANKSGIVING
For Our Future Inheritance

Beloved, now are we the sons of God, and it doth not yet appear what we shall be: but we know that, when He shall appear, we shall be like Him; for we shall see Him as He is (1 John 3:2).

Though we are enriched by reflecting on our past heritage and thrilled when we consider the blessings that envelop our daily lives, for the child of God the *best is yet to come.* Heaven! Think of it—an eternity at home with our Lord.

Heaven is not some myth, nor is it a figment of the human imagination. It is as sure as the promises of God in the Scriptures:

I go to prepare a place for you. And if I go and prepare a place for you, I will come again, and receive you unto Myself; that where I am, there ye may be also (John 14:2, 3).

As it is written, eye hath not seen, nor ear heard, neither have entered into the heart of man, the things which God hath prepared for them that love Him (1 Corinthians 2:9).

In this day of the disposable and the temporary, Christians must live according to their belief in eternity. The apostle Paul reminded the believers at Corinth that if their hope in Christ was only related to this life, they would be the most miserable of all men (1 Cor. 15:19). The anticipation of God's tomorrow makes it possible for Christians to live victoriously and joyfully today regardless of life's circumstances. A joyous faith realizes that at best one sees through the glass dimly, and that we must accept by faith the ways of a sovereign God. We look for the day when that imperfect faith will be rewarded with sight:

For now we see through a glass, darkly; but then face to face; now I know in part: but then shall I know even as also I am known (1 Corinthians 13:12).

What will heaven be like? Golden streets? Jasper walls?

Crystal seas? Jeweled crowns? Certainly, but much, much more. No mortal mind can fully assimilate the concept of heaven. It is impossible to describe heavenly scenes with earthly symbols. One of the prime occupations of heaven can be understood, however, because we are preparing for it now—the worship and praise of our Lord. Singing will continue to be one of the sublime enjoyments throughout eternity. One of the heavenly chorus anthems we'll sing could well be:

Thou art worthy, O Lord, to receive glory and honor and power; for Thou hast created all things, and for Thy pleasure they are and were created (Revelation 4:11).

Until that day, however, may we know in part the joy of glorifying God as we join our voices in praise and thanksgiving to the One who made it possible for us to sing eternally.

Think of stepping on shore, and finding it heaven!
Of taking hold of a hand, and finding it God's hand,
Of breathing new air, and finding it celestial air,
Of feeling invigorated, and finding it immortality,
Of passing from storm and tempest to an unbroken calm,
Of waking up, and finding it Home!   —Anonymous

GROUP DISCUSSION

What concepts does the word "heaven" invoke in your thinking? Is it possible to become so heavenly minded that we become of no earthly good here and now? How can we maintain a proper balance between the heavenly hope and our present ministries?

SUGGESTED GROUP SINGING

The Sands of Time Are Sinking, No. 93—*101 Hymn Stories*
Beyond the Sunset, No. 12—*101 More Hymn Stories*

THOUGHT

Nobody dreams of music in hell, and nobody conceives of heaven without it.

PEOPLE OF PRAISE AND THANKSGIVING
Knowing and Doing

I will sing of the mercies of the Lord forever: with my mouth will I make known Thy faithfulness to all generations (Psalm 89:1).

Most believers in Christ would readily agree that the Christian life should be characterized by words such as "joy," "praise," and "thankful." We easily forget, however, the daily disciplines and practices that a life of praise and thanksgiving requires.

Our lack of praise and thanksgiving can be likened to the response of the ten lepers after being healed by Christ (Luke 17:11-19), with only one returning to express praise and thanks. It is interesting to imagine the life-long remorse that characterized the nine ungrateful lives.

I meant to be back, but you may guess
I was filled with amazement I cannot express
To think that after those horrible years,
That passion of loathing and passion of fears,
Of sores unendurable—eaten, defiled—
My flesh was as smooth as the flesh of a child.
I was drunken with joy; I was crazy with glee;
I scarcely could walk and I scarcely could see,
For the dazzle of sunshine where all had been black;
But I meant to go back, Oh, I meant to go back!
I had thought to return, when my people came out,
There were tears of rejoicing and laughter and shout;
My cup was so full I seemed nothing to lack!
But I meant to go back, Oh, I meant to go back!

Anonymous

Praise and thanksgiving should be the natural response from God's people for His daily blessings of life. To help choir members recall these truths more vividly, acrostics based on the words PRAISE and THANKSGIVING are used. Perhaps the choir members can think of other principles and blessings suggested by these letters that will aid in translating such concepts into "thanksliving."

P—Do it personally. Must be an individual experience

R—Do it repeatedly. Must become a daily way of life

A—Do it affectionately. Must be done emotionally—not just as a routine habit

I—Do it intelligently. Must be done thoughtfully—not in a vague, sentimental fashion

S—Do it spiritually. Must be done out of an intimate relationship with the Lord

E—Do it as a preparation for eternity. Must be done in the light of our future occupation in heaven

T—Treasure, the income and savings we have

H—Homes, the places God has given us in which to dwell

A—Assurance, that we are members of God's family

N—New life, the gift from above

K—Kindness, showered on us by God and His people

S—Singing, as a means of expressing our joy

G—Grace, bestowed liberally and sufficiently for every need

I—Intellect, with which to know and learn about God

V—Victory, over sin by the power of the Holy Spirit

I—Insight, into the truths of God's Word

N—Nearness, God is with us in every experience of life

G—Giving, a tangible means of thanking Him for His blessings

GROUP DISCUSSION

What are some major hindrances to a lifestyle of praise and thanksgiving?

SUGGESTED GROUP SINGING

Now Thank We All Our God, No. 62—*101 Hymn Stories*

THOUGHT

A thankful heart is not only the greatest virtue, but the parent of all the other virtues.   —Cicero

THE SONGS OF CHRISTMAS
The Song of Mary—"The Magnificat"

*My soul doth magnify the Lord, and my spirit hath rejoiced in God
my Savior (Luke 1:46, 47).*

The songs of the Christmas season, songs about Christ's
birth, represent some of the finest music known to man. One of
the choicest collections of sacred music for the Christmas
season is George Fredrick Handel's immortal *Messiah.* Handel
began writing the music for this biblical text in 1741, and he
completed all 53 numbers in just 24 days. *The Messiah,*
presented on April 13, 1742, is undoubtedly the most frequently
performed oratorio ever written, and it is certainly one of the
most highly esteemed. At the first London performance, when
the chorus began the word "hallelujah," King George II was so
inspired that he stood to his feet. Audiences stand today when
the inspiring "Hallelujah Chorus" is heard.

Another musical master of this period is Johann Sebastian
Bach (1685-1750). Often called "the father of church music," he
wrote two great Christmas works: *The Magnificat* and the
Christmas Oratorio. Both of these are still frequently performed.

The New Testament contains four important "songs" related
to the Christmas message. They are:

THE SONG OF MARY—"The Magnificat"

THE SONG OF ZACHARIAS—"The Benedictus"

THE SONG OF SIMEON—"The Nunc Dimittis"

THE SONG OF THE ANGELS—"Gloria in Excelsis Deo"

In addition to providing the basis for many great musical
works, each of these texts contains important spiritual lessons
for us today.

The Magnificat. The song of Mary begins with an outburst
of praise to God. The language of her song is Old Testament,
showing Mary to be a girl familiar with the Scriptures. Her

34

poetic statement, perhaps composed on her journey to visit Elizabeth, is a humble contemplation of the mercies of God. It resembles Hannah's prayer of rejoicing over the birth of her son, Samuel (1 Sam. 2:1). Mary's song is named "The Magnificat," which is the first word of the Latin version, *Magnificat anima mea Dominum.* It may be divided into four stanzas:

*The first (Luke 1:46-48) is an expression of highest praise to God for what He had done for His handmaiden. When she said "God, my Savior," she confessed the truth that she too had to know Christ not only as an earthly Son but as her own personal Savior.

*The second (vv. 49, 50) broadens out to acknowledge God's power, holiness, and mercy to all generations.

*The third (vv. 51-53) is prophetic in tone, describing how God will bring down the proud and exalt the humble.

*The fourth (vv. 54-55) focuses upon God's help for His people and the remembrance of His covenant.

We marvel at the faith of this Jewish young woman and stand in awe and respect at her knowledge of the Lord. No wonder she rejoiced (v. 47) at the angel's announcement that she would bring the Messiah, the Son of God, into this world. And from henceforth all generations would call her blessed (v. 48).

GROUP DISCUSSION
What song of the Christmas season has been especially meaningful to you? Why?

SUGGESTED GROUP SINGING
Silent Night! Holy Night!, No. 80—*101 Hymn Stories*

THOUGHT
He became what we are in order that we might become as He is.   —Athanasius

PEOPLE OF PRAISE AND THANKSGIVING
The Song of Zacharias—"The Benedictus"

Blessed be the Lord God of Israel; for He hath visited and redeemed His people (Luke 1:68).

An aged priest walks slowly toward the golden altar. Two priests accompany him, one carrying a golden bowl filled with live coals, the other a similar bowl filled with incense. The priest, Zacharias, is nearly overcome with emotion, for he has been selected by lot to perform this special mission. This is the only time during his life that he will have this awesome privilege. A hush falls over the sanctuary as he enters the holy place and spreads the incense over the coals. The people wait for him to emerge, but he does not appear. An angel has come to tell him that he will father the forerunner of the promised Messiah! Zacharias is struck dumb until the child's birth.

The prophecy seems impossible, for Zacharias and his wife are old and childless. Yet it's true! They are going to have a child! And when their son is born, there is great rejoicing. When the baby is eight days old, he is taken to the temple for circumcision. Elizabeth insists that his name be John. The people disagree, for the family has never used that name. They turn to Zacharias, and he writes, "His name shall be John." Immediately, his speech returns, and he begins to sing praise to the Lord. His song, recorded in Scripture, is known as "Benedictus," because that is the first word of its Latin title.

Spoken under the direction of the Holy Spirit (Luke 1:67), the words of Zacharias's song are a prophecy. *The Benedictus* may be divided into four stanzas:

Thanksgiving for the Messiah (vv. 68-70). God has looked upon His people and is providing redemption for them. The promised Messiah is a descendant of King David and the fulfillment of Old Testament prophecies.

The Great Deliverance (vv. 71-75). The Messiah will be a

36

deliverer (v. 71), and provider of mercy. He came in fulfillment of the covenants, particularly the covenant made with
Abraham (Genesis 12:1-3). The benefactors will serve Him
with fear and holiness.

* *The Role of John* (vv. 76, 77). The mission of Zacharias's
son is then summarized. These promises are addressed
directly to the little child, and they echo two Old Testament
prophecies: Isaiah 40:3; Malachi 3:1. The fact that he is
called a prophet is astounding, for Israel has not had a
prophet for four centuries.

* *The Messiah's Salvation* (vv. 78, 79). The salvation the
Messiah brings will come through God's tender mercy. The
promised Redeemer is described as a rising sun who will
shine on those who walk in darkness (v. 78). He will bring
peace to His people (v. 79).

Although Zacharias's song has Jewish political overtones, it
is solidly spiritual in nature—an outburst of prophecy and
praise from a devoted priest whose life was blessed beyond
measure.

Come and worship, come and worship, worship Christ,
the new-born King. —James Montgomery

GROUP DISCUSSION
Discuss the importance of John the Baptist's role as a prophet
and forerunner in God's redemptive plan. Share an experience
in which you were awed as was Zacharias at the workings of
God on your behalf.

SUGGESTED GROUP SINGING
Hark! the Herald Angels Sing, No. 31—*101 More Hymn
Stories*
It Came Upon the Midnight Clear, No. 47—*101 More Hymn
Stories*

THOUGHT
Christmas began in the heart of God. It is complete only when it
reaches the heart of man.

THE SONGS OF CHRISTMAS
The Song of Simeon—"The Nunc Dimittis"

Lord, now lettest thou Thy servant depart in peace, according to Thy Word: For mine eyes have seen Thy salvation (Luke 2:29, 30).

The "Nunc Dimittis" was sung in the temple on the day the infant Son of Mary was presented to the priest, according to Jewish custom. The singer was Simeon, and its theme is one of joyful submission to God, the Sovereign Master.

Everything we know about Simeon is recorded in this brief passage. He lived in Jerusalem, was righteous and devout, and longed for the coming of the Messiah, often referred to as "The Consolation of Israel." He was probably a layman rather than a temple priest.

Simeon was one who was sensitive to the Holy Spirit's leading in his life. The Spirit, in fact, had revealed to him that he would not die until he saw "the Lord's Christ." Imagine the anticipation that must have filled his heart! The master artists throughout history pictured Simeon as an old man, though we are given no indication of this in the Bible.

He was led by the Holy Spirit to the temple the very day that Mary and Joseph brought Jesus, again showing his submission to the Spirit's leading. When the parents entered, Simeon took the child into his arms. The Holy Spirit had revealed to him that this was the long-promised Messiah. Simeon's heart was overflowing with gratitude, for we are told that he "blessed God."

The first words of Simeon's song indicate that he knew his release from life had come. Here was the Messiah! Now he could die in peace. The anticipation, the wondering, the concern were finished. He believed implicitly the Holy Spirit's message that the child before him would bring God's salvation to all mankind.

The Nunc Dimittis reaches out farther than either that of Mary or Zacharias. Mary saw Christ as a personal Savior;

Zacharias saw the child as Israel's national Messiah-deliverer. Simeon, however, saw Him as the One who had come not only for Israel, but for all people. To the Gentile, still stumbling in spiritual darkness, He was *light*. To Israel, who had so many advantages but still followed their own way, He was *glory*. This gives Simeon's song a prophetic element, for Israel's ultimate glory yet awaits the day of her salvation at the coming again of the Savior.

Simeon then turned to bless Mary and Joseph, who were astonished at what he had said about Jesus. But not all of Simeon's words were happy, for he identified Jesus as the One who would divide Israel spiritually. His concluding words, that a sword would pierce Mary's heart, were fulfilled at Calvary.

> O come to my heart, Lord Jesus—There is room in my heart for Thee!
> My heart shall rejoice, Lord Jesus, when Thou comest and callest for me! —Emily E.S. Elliott

GROUP DISCUSSION

In what ways is Jesus the light of the Gentiles? How is the fact that Simeon could now die in peace similar to the Christian's experience? What sorrow and anguish did Mary experience at the cross?

SUGGESTED GROUP SINGING

While Shepherds Watched Their Flocks, No. 101—*101 Hymn Stories*
Joy to the World!, No. 52—*101 More Hymn Stories*

THOUGHT

Christmas: not the tinsel, not the giving and receiving, not even the carols. Rather, it is the humble heart that receives anew God's wondrous gift, the Christ.

THE SONGS OF CHRISTMAS
The Song of the Angels—"Gloria in Excelsis Deo"

Glory to God in the highest, and on earth peace, good will toward men (Luke 2:14).

Did you notice the wonderful progression in the songs of Christmas that we have been considering this month? The Song of Mary is an expression of praise to the Lord for her favored privilege and for her vision of God as Israel's helper in time of need. The scope widened with Zacharias, whose song extolls the Messiah as Israel's Redeemer and King. Simeon's song is world-embracing, for he envisions the Messiah as the glory of Israel and the light of the Gentiles. Finally, the song of the angels offers glory to God and peace and good will toward all the earth.

With striking suddenness, the tranquility of the Judean hillside was interrupted by the appearance of an angel of the Lord. The glory of the Lord flashed brilliantly, and to a lowly band of shepherds came the message from the heavenly host (Luke 2:8-14). It contained these elements:

*Exhortation—The shepherds were told to stop being frightened.

*Announcement—"I bring you good news," the angel proclaimed.

*Rejoicing—The news was "of great joy," for the solution to the world's greatest problem—sin—was about to be unfolded.

*Scope—All people, regardless of race, sex, education, social position, or age would benefit by Messiah's coming.

*The Event—Next, the immediate cause for rejoicing was revealed. On that very day, in David's town, a baby was born who would bring deliverance to all who would believe.

*The Identification—The One whose birth was heralded that

day was identified as the Savior, Christ the Lord. This is the only place in the Synoptic Gospels that Jesus is called "Savior," highlighting His purpose to bring redemption from sin. Then a sign was given; He would be swaddled (bundled) in blankets and lying in a manger.

The Angelic Response—Then the curtain of night was drawn back, and the heavens were filled with angels, whose voices joined in a mighty chorus of praise to God and peace to men of God's good pleasure.

After the angels left the wondering shepherds, without hesitation they went to Bethlehem, found the infant, verified the story, and went out to proclaim the good news to all who would hear.

And now, twenty centuries later, we have seen in history and in the response from our own hearts that the angels' message was true. We too have the responsibility of sharing this good news as expressed in Psalm 78:4-7.

The wonderful story our fathers made known,
To children succeeding by us must be known.

GROUP DISCUSSION

What particular event in the Christmas narrative seems especially significant to you? In what sense is the church choir's ministry an extension of the angels' song?

SUGGESTED GROUP SINGING

Angels From the Realms of Glory, No. 7—*101 Hymn Stories*

THOUGHT

Nearly 20 long centuries have passed since Jesus' birth. Yet more words have been written about this Babe, more pictures painted, more music composed than for any other person who ever lived. Truly, He is the Son of God!

LESSONS FROM THE NEW TESTAMENT
Early Christian Worship

Who shall separate us from the love of Christ? Shall tribulation, or distress, or persecution, . . . Nay, in all these things we are more than conquerors through Him who loved us (Romans 8:35, 37).

First-century Christians continued to use the temple and synagogues for their places of worship, but they preferred to have the simple love feasts and communion services in their homes (Acts 2:46). The traditional chanting, antiphonal psalm-singing, and other Old Testament musical practices no doubt were still known and were part of the worship of these early believers.

For the first several centuries the early church suffered periods of severe persecution by the Roman Empire, forcing these believers ("followers of the way") to assemble secretly in homes or to hide in catacombs. Several key dates, events, and personalities of these centuries are:

A.D. 54-68—Emperor Nero's reign. The first real persecution of the early Christians.

c. 56—The apostle Paul's letter to the church at Rome. (Read this book in the light of the persecution of early believers.)

70—The destruction of the temple in Jerusalem and the dispersion of the Jews.

313—Christianity legalized throughout the Roman Empire during the reign of Constantine I, "The Great." This era is known as "the peace of the church."

381—Christianity was made the official religion of the state. The beginning of phenomenal church growth.

354-430—St. Augustine. Next to the apostle Paul, Augustine was considered the most influential early-church leader. His writings, "Confessions" and "The City of God," were important in establishing church doctrines.

340?-397—St. Ambrose, Bishop of Milan. He encouraged congregational singing to combat many doctrinal errors prevalent at this time. Shortly, however, a church council decreed: "If laymen are not to interpret the Scriptures for themselves, so they are not to sing the songs of the church."

540-604—Pope Gregory. An important developer and organizer of the church's music. Gregorian chants became the basis of Catholic church music and the church's liturgy, the Mass.

All early church music was vocal, for instrumental music was associated with Roman paganism. The text rather than the music was all-important. Monody or solo music was the most important, musical development. Monody is also described as plain song, plain chant, and Gregorian chant. These chants were borrowed from the earlier Hebrew temple-synagogue services, and they consisted mainly of intoning the psalms. The non-psalm biblical texts were called "canticles." The music of the church increasingly became the music of the clergy. This led to the development of music as an artform in the Catholic church, but it ruled out lay participation in congregational singing.

New Testament references to the music ministry are limited to the apostle Paul's letters to the churches at Ephesus and Colosse (Eph. 5:19 and Col. 3:16). These passages teach that the early New Testament believers, despite their hardships and persecutions, were to sing *psalms, hymns,* and *spiritual songs.*

GROUP DISCUSSION
What is lost in Christian experience if congregational singing is excluded today? If the music of the church becomes mainly "special music?"

SUGGESTED GROUP SINGING
O God, Our Help in Ages Past, No. 66—*101 Hymn Stories*

THOUGHT
We are the personification of the things we believe in and for which we would die.

LESSONS FROM THE NEW TESTAMENT
Sing Psalms

... be filled with the Spirit: Speaking to yourselves in psalms and hymns and spiritual songs, singing and making melody in your heart to the Lord (Ephesians 5:18, 19).

Although New Testament references to the use of church music are relatively few, much can be learned from the scriptural instructions that have been given. From the letter to the church of Ephesus (5:18, 19) can be gleaned these truths:

*A joyful life is directly related to being "filled with the Spirit."

*New Testament believers were to be active participants in praising God, not passive spectators.

*The psalms, hymns, and spiritual songs should minister to us spiritually. A parallel verse, Colossians 3:16, teaches that we're also to use these musical forms in ministering to others. Church music, then, must always be thought of as a ministry and not mere entertainment (James 5:13).

*Our musical expressions are to be directed "to the Lord." Singers must always have a God-focus when ministering.

*Our songs should produce a joyous effect. It has been well said that if there were more singing Christians, there would be more Christians.

*Our music ministry should employ a balance of musical styles as represented by "psalms, hymns, and spiritual songs."

Most likely some first-century believers questioned whether the Old Testament songs, the psalms, were still appropriate for New Testament worship. The word "psalms" implies more than just the 150 psalms, but rather any of the exalted expressions of praise found throughout the Old Testament. The apostle Paul made it clear that New Testament Christians were not to neglect this great heritage. Without these reminders of God's majesty and power that appear in the psalms and other Old Testament scriptures, believers tend to limit God to their own experience and understanding. Every generation needs to hear repeatedly the psalmist's perspective of God and his views of man and eternity—that the Eternal God is ever worthy of man's worship, praise, and service.

The psalms can rightly be thought of as the enduring expressions or the great traditional classics of sacred music. How our hearts are thrilled and our spirits soar when the "Hallelujah Chorus" and similar inspiring anthems of praise are heard. Every congregation needs spiritual moments such as these. Therefore, with the apostle Paul we echo, DON'T NEGLECT THE SINGING OF PSALMS!

> The King of love my Shepherd is, whose goodness faileth never;
> I nothing lack, if I am His and He is mine forever.
>
> And so thru all the length of days, Thy goodness faileth never;
> Good Shepherd, may I sing Thy praise, within Thy house forever.　　　　—From Psalm 23—Henry W. Baker

GROUP DISCUSSION

What does the expression "filled with the Spirit" mean to you? What suggestions can you offer for the music program of this church to encourage a more significant ministry to ourselves and to others?

SUGGESTED GROUP SINGING

Jesus Shall Reign, No. 48— *101 Hymn Stories*
Surely Goodness and Mercy, No. 80—*101 More Hymn Stories*

THOUGHT

God's work of creating is done; our work of praising has just begun.

LESSONS FROM THE NEW TESTAMENT
Sing Hymns

Let the Word of Christ dwell in you richly in all wisdom; teaching and admonishing one another in psalms and hymns and spiritual songs, singing with grace in your hearts to the Lord (Colossians 3:16).

From Colossians 3:16, which is parallel to Ephesians 5:18, 19, one can readily see that the apostle Paul had a singleness of mind regarding the use of music in the New Testament churches. Note the lessons to be learned from this verse:

*A joyful life is directly related to the prominence the Scriptures are given in one's life.

*Our musical expressions are to be a ministry to others. The singers are to instruct and encourage one another by this means. (How important that our songs communicate God's truths accurately!)

*Our music ministry should employ a balance of styles—psalms, hymns, and spiritual songs.

*Songs must be based upon the personal experience of God's grace in one's life.

*Singers must always have their songs directed "to the Lord."

Evangelical Christians have rightly been called the "people of the Book." It could be stated, however, that we are really the people of two books, the Bible and the hymnal. Throughout Protestant history the hymnal has been the most important and widely used book, except the Bible, in the worship of God.

For first-century Christians, hymns were newer religious expressions that extolled the works and teachings of Christ. They also conveyed the emerging New Testament doctrines and spiritual applications of the newly-founded Christian faith. The following Scriptures are believed to have been hymn-texts in their earliest form that were sung by the congregations: Eph. 5:14; 1 Tim. 3:16; 4:15, 16; 2 Tim. 2:11-13; Titus 3:14.

46

In the fourth century, Augustine described a hymn as follows:

Do you know what a hymn is? It is singing to the praise of God. If you praise God and do not sing, you utter no hymn. If you sing and praise not God, you utter no hymn. If you praise anything which does not pertain to the praise of God, though in singing you praise, you utter no hymn.

The church hymnal should occupy a significant place in every area of a Christian's life—at corporate worship, in the Christian education of children, and in family and personal devotions. Much of our spiritual learning and growth is the result of the hymns we sing. Therefore, with the apostle Paul we echo, DON'T NEGLECT THE SINGING OF HYMNS!

When morning gilds the skies, my heart awaking cries:
    May Jesus Christ be praised!
Alike at work and prayer, to Jesus I repair:
    May Jesus Christ be praised!
                    —German hymn. Translated by Edward Caswall

GROUP DISCUSSION
Make a conscientious effort this week to use your church hymnal as part of your personal and family devotions. Rediscover the truths of several of your favorite hymns. If possible, read the background of the hymns and the experiences that prompted their writing. Be ready to share some of your discoveries.

SUGGESTED GROUP SINGING
Great Is Thy Faithfulness, No. 27—*101 Hymn Stories*
Our Great Savior, No. 73—*101 More Hymn Stories*

THOUGHT
After more than 60 years of almost daily reading of the Bible, I never fail to find it always new and marvellously in tune with the changing needs of every day.   —Cecil B. DeMille

LESSONS FROM THE NEW TESTAMENT
Sing Spiritual Songs

I will pray with the Spirit, and I will pray with the understanding also; I will sing with the Spirit, and I will sing with the understanding also (1 Corinthians 14:15).

This is one of the few verses in the New Testament that tells about the use of music in the church. We see:

1. *The apostle Paul reminded the Corinthians to be actively engaged in two important spiritual activities—PRAYING AND PRAISING.*

2. *Though both of these activities should be under the influence of the Holy Spirit, implying a response of spontaneity and warmth, yet both must be done rationally— they must be products of the mind as well as of the Spirit. Valid spiritual experiences must always maintain this proper balance between the emotional and the mental.*

For the first-century believers, spiritual songs were spontaneous expressions that arose from their personal, often ecstatic experiences with God. They were generally performed in solo form with a great deal of improvisation, perhaps on a single syllable of a word such as "alleluia."

These spiritual songs could well be thought of as a counterpart of today's gospel songs. Gospel music began in America shortly after the close of the Civil War, and it has evolved into a number of popular musical styles. These songs are not meant to be great enduring sacred classics, nor are they intended to be the profound teaching hymns of the church. Even so, some do become lasting favorites. For example, "The Old Rugged Cross." Gospel songs should be thought of as the "now" expressions of believers or the "folk" music of the church. They are sometimes even called the "disposable music" of the church. Yet these songs allow believers, especially young people, to express feelings about God and His leading in their lives in a very personal manner. A proper balance of worthy gospel songs in the music ministry of a church will give a freshness and vitality to a church program.

Has God given you a talent for expressing spiritual feelings and truths with words and music? This gift can be a strong influence in the spread of the gospel. The use of original spiritual songs will often be the spark that ignites a spiritual renewal when ministered in a local assembly. These expressions are not written for monetary gain or for the purpose of maintaining a professional reputation, but simply as grateful responses to the indisputable hand of God upon a person's life.

Our hymnals, then, should contain a sound balance of traditional psalm-classics, doctrinal hymns, and experiential spiritual songs. It would be good if our hymnals also had a section of blank pages so that the books could be an ever-growing collection, to include new spiritual expressions arising from the local congregation. The deep, spiritual experiences of believers of the past should be happening among Christians today, prompting new expressions of the ageless truths of God. Therefore, with the apostle Paul we echo, DON'T NEGLECT THE SINGING OF SPIRITUAL SONGS!

GROUP DISCUSSION

One of the controversial areas in some evangelical churches is the use of contemporary gospel songs in the services. When, where, and how do you feel these songs should be used? What about the use of sound tracks or rhythm instruments with these songs?

SUGGESTED GROUP SINGING

I'd Rather Have Jesus, No. 42—*101 More Hymn Stories*

THOUGHT

He who knows not the language of praise cannot speak of true happiness.

THE LOCAL CHURCH
Its Purpose

Upon this rock I will build My church, and the gates of hell shall not prevail against it (Matthew 16:18).

The *church universal,* believers in Christ from every age and culture, and the *church local,* individual congregations of redeemed people, have been chosen by God to accomplish His earthly purpose—calling out a people to represent Him, and with whom He can share eternity. The promise of Christ is that nothing—not even the gates of hell—will thwart that purpose or the ultimate triumph of His church.

The first account of a New Testament church is given in Acts 2:41-47. From this Scripture the following purposes for a local church can be gained:

The Local Church Worships Together.
> They continued steadfastly in doctrine, fellowship, breaking bread, praying, and praising (vv. 42, 46, 47).

The Local Church Evangelizes Together.
> Three thousand responded, were baptized, and were added to the church. Other persons were added daily as they were saved (vv. 41, 47).

> Their leaders ministered with power and spiritual authority. Reverential awe came upon everyone, and spiritual wonders were demonstrated by the apostles (v. 43).

The Local Church Learns Truth Together.
> They remained true to the apostles' doctrine (v. 42).

The Local Church Fellowships Together.
> They had all things in common and were strongly unified (vv. 44, 46).

The Local Church Reaches Out Together.
> They shared their wealth with those in need (v. 45).

These dynamic practices of the local church at Jerusalem

following the day of Pentecost are valid guidelines for local churches today. In a time when many churches have neglected their spiritual mandates, when they no longer seem effective in reaching and transforming lives, and when many members have become lethargic and disenchanted, it is imperative that concerned leaders renew their commitment to God's spiritual purposes for this world through His chosen agency, the CHURCH.

May a renewed commitment cause us to say with conviction,

LET GOD BE GOD,
LET THE CHURCH BE THE CHURCH,
LET HIS PEOPLE REJOICE!

Like a mighty army moves the Church of God;
Brothers, we are treading where the saints have trod.
We are not divided, all one body we—
One in hope and doctrine, one in charity.

Onward, Christian soldiers, marching as to war,
With the cross of Jesus going on before.

—Sabine Baring-Gould

GROUP DISCUSSION

Why is it important that Christians have a biblical and balanced view of both the Church universal and the local church? Is it possible for a local church to be involved in worthy activities that do not relate to the scriptural purposes listed?

SUGGESTED GROUP SINGING

I Love Thy Kngdom, Lord, No. 36—*101 Hymn Stories*
The Church's One Foundation, No. 88—*101 Hymn Stories*

THOUGHT

The church is not a gallery for the exhibition of eminent Christians, but a school for the education of imperfect ones.

—Henry Ward Beecher

THE LOCAL CHURCH
The Role of Music

And He gave some, apostles; and some, prophets; and some, evangelists; and some, pastors and teachers; for the perfecting of the saints, for the work of the ministry, for the edifying of the body of Christ (Ephesians 4:11, 12)

Concerned local church leaders will earnestly pursue these scriptural purposes for their assembly by providing

* *Worship for Believers*—promoting the infinite worth of God with appropriate proclamations of that worth.

* *Evangelism for Unbelievers*—proclaiming the essential biblical truths that affect one's eternal destiny and urge personal decision and commitment.

* *Instruction for All Believers*—Christian education that involves teaching, discipling, nurturing, training, and communicating biblical truth to every age group.

* *Fellowship for All Believers*—developing the "body" relationships of caring and sharing in Christian love.

* *A Living Representation of God*—demonstrating to the local community God's concern for the total needs of individuals.

We must diligently desire to direct the music ministry of the local church to accomplish these goals.

* *Worship and Music.* Music heightens our God consciousness. Although beauty is not synonymous with true worship, there is a strong relationship between our aesthetic and spiritual responses. Beginning with the strains of the prelude, the congregational singing, and the blended voices of a choir, music lifts the worshiper into the presence of God.

* *Evangelism and Music.* Music prepares the listener for the spoken Word. For many believers, a song has directly

influenced them in knowing God. All important evangelistic movements in church history have been accompanied by a revival of sacred music.

Instruction and Music. Music helps us learn basic spiritual truths. The insights that direct our daily lives have often been learned through songs in early childhood. The music and Christian education ministries are closely allied.

Fellowship and Music. Music unifies people. Making music together changes people from merely a collection of individuals into a unified congregation or choir.

Social Concern and Music. Music promotes a benevolent spirit. The truths of sacred songs penetrate and motivate our social consciousness. We become people-oriented and better able to minister to the whole person.

Church music, then, is a functional art. It is meant to serve the purposes of God and His church. As noble an artform as music is, it does not exist for its own sake within the church program. Rather, it is one of the most vital means available for the local assembly to achieve its God-given objectives. The validity of sacred music must ultimately be judged by whether it helps the local church accomplish its scriptural purposes, glorifies God, and edifies His people.

GROUP DISCUSSION

Give examples of how music relates to each of the scriptural purposes of the local church. Evaluate the strengths and weaknesses of this local church in accomplishing these scriptural purposes. Give positive, constructive suggestions for improvement.

SUGGESTED GROUP SINGING

Come, Thou Almighty King, No. 14—*101 Hymn Stories*
How Great Thou Art, No. 33—*101 Hymn Stories*

THOUGHT

God does not comfort us to make us comfortable, but to make us comforters.

THE LOCAL CHURCH
The Adult Choir

Now there are diversities of gifts, but the same Spirit. For as the body is one, and hath many members, and all the members of that one body, being many, are one body: so also is Christ (1 Corinthians 12:4, 12).

Every believer has been given at least one spiritual gift (ability) to assist the local church in achieving its God-given purposes (1 Peter 4:10). The goal of local church leadership is to encourage every able-bodied member to realize and develop his gift and to become actively involved in its use. An inactive believer is not only a deterrent to his church's mission, but he is also a detriment to his own spiritual growth and well-being.

Music is not mentioned in the New Testament as one of the spiritual gifts; even so, the implication is that it is because it is such an integral part of the church's scriptural purposes. The music group that can give the strongest support to the church's ministry is the adult choir, which group epitomizes the efforts of the entire music program. The goal of younger church singers should be eventual membership in the senior choir. The choir members should be the most spiritual, loyal, and thoroughly trained of all the church's musicians.

An effective adult choir, comprising approximately ten percent of the active church membership, can make a strong contribution to the ministry of the local church because:

*It offers a more exalted expression of praise to God than can be given by the congregation.

*It provides a supportive force of leadership for a public service as leaders of enthusiastic congregational singing, responsive Scriptural readings, and as examples of attentiveness to the spoken Word.

*It demonstrates, to the congregation, the proper attitudes of worship as expressed in this verse, "That thou mayest know how thou oughtest to behave thyself in the house of God, which is the church of the living God, the pillar and ground of the truth" (1 Timothy 3:15).

*It represents the important New Testament truth of the priesthood of the believer—lay people who are actively involved in the worship and praise of God.

*It supplies the church with a core of people who, because of their position of leadership, are vitally concerned about their Christian witness and daily lifestyle.

*It affords opportunities for unusual spiritual growth and fellowship for the individual members.

Singing in an adult choir, then, is more than merely preparing a new special number each week. It is the building up of the body of Christ with the use of God-given spiritual gifts. A privilege, yes—but also a solemn responsibility!

> God sent His singers upon the earth
> With songs of sadness and of mirth,
> That they might touch the hearts of men
> And bring them back to heaven again.
> —Henry Wadsworth Longfellow

GROUP DISCUSSION

How does a Christian discover his/her spiritual gift? In what ways could a Christian enjoy a natural talent and not be using it as a spiritual gift? In what ways has the past year's choir experience made a spiritual contribution to your growth and well-being?

SUGGESTED GROUP SINGING

All Creatures of Our God and King, No. 3—*101 Hymn Stories*

THOUGHT

In God's service, our abilities must begin with a humble attitude of availability.

THE LOCAL CHURCH
Graded Choirs

Suffer the little children to come unto Me, and forbid them not; for of such is the kingdom of God (Mark 10:14).

Children and youth are the prized possessions of any local church. As concerned music leaders, we must exert every effort to make our highest priority the teaching and training of the young in the ways of God. Christ was a prime example of this concern throughout His earthly ministry. Despite the pressures of ministering to the multitudes, He had time to invite youngsters to Himself.

Christian leaders long have realized that music is one of the most effective ways to bring spiritual truths and concepts into the hearts and minds of children and youth. Many of our gospel hymns were written for this specific purpose. The influence of secular music on today's youth is unquestioned. When music is properly administered in the church, it represents one of the finest opportunities in the entire Christian education program to reach and teach children and teen-agers.

As those who have experienced the values of church music, adult choir members should be the most ardent promoters and supporters of a graded choir ministry.

A graded choir program ensures that there are opportunities for every age group to be ministered to, as well as to minister, through music. A long-range goal for a graded choir program would include such groups as a beginner's choir, ages 4 and 5; a primary choir, grades 1 through 3; a junior choir, grades 4 through 6. There should also be an active teen program that includes vocal, instrumental, and dramatic activities. A vital music program will do much to ensure the success of a local church's endeavors in the Christian education and youth ministries.

A graded church choir program has many benefits, including these:

It Perpetuates Church Music. If there are to be better trained adult singers and congregations with a greater understanding and appreciation of the music ministry, this training must begin with the youth.

It Enriches a Child's Life. Music is natural and emotionally satisfying for children and youth. The average youngster will thoroughly enjoy and respond to music that is presented properly.

It Ministers Spiritually to the Child. A dedicated music director working with youth can make a profound impact on the individual. He/she will seek to lead each youngster to a personal relationship with God, develop proper concepts of worship, prepare each member for a lifetime of Christian service, and demonstrate the richness of wholesome Christian fellowship.

Although not everyone is musically gifted or able to sing tunefully, every believer, both young and old, should be given an opportunity to respond with joyful sounds unto the Lord. Silent Christians soon become stagnant Christians.

Stand up and bless the Lord, ye people of His choice;
Stand up and bless the Lord your God, with heart and soul and voice.   —James Montgomery

GROUP DISCUSSION
Do you feel that this church has an effective music ministry with its children and teens? Make positive suggestions for improving these areas of ministry with the children, youth, and teens.

SUGGESTED GROUP SINGING
Jesus Loves Me, No. 47—*101 Hymn Stories*
When He Cometh, No. 97—*101 More Hymn Stories*

THOUGHT
Every child has a right to be both well fed and well led.

THE WORSHIP SERVICE
Its Importance

Get thee behind Me, Satan; for it is written, Thou shalt worship the Lord thy God, and Him only shalt thou serve (Luke 4:8).

One of the unchanging commands of Scripture is the command to worship God. In our sinfulness we are inclined to make something or someone other than God Himself the object of worship. Even Jesus was tempted by Satan to worship falsely. Yet Christ responded by stating forcefully the dominant theme of the Old Testament—that God alone must be worshiped and served. There can be no other God!

The act of worship implies communion and fellowship. The eternal, infinite God desires communion with man, and finite man in turn is capable of fellowshipping with the living God. Our concept of Him should be ever-expanding as we grow in grace and in knowledge of Him. Compare this relationship with a child's devotion to his parents. In the earliest years, this devotion is based primarily on the parent's ability to fulfill the child's needs. By the time he reaches young adulthood, however, the child will normally have developed a deep appreciation of his parents, simply for who and what they are. Spiritually, we too must mature in our understanding of God and in our appreciation of Him. We must worship God not merely for what He has or is doing in our individual lives, as important as that is, but above all for Who He is—His being, character, and works.

Trying to define what we sense and feel in the worship experience is difficult, and it is not the same for everyone. Consider these different aspects. Worship is:

*An absorption with God rather than with self.

*An adoring attitude toward the person, attributes, and acts of a transcendent God, and a willful desire to conform to Him through obedience to His revealed will.

*An act by a redeemed man, the creature, toward God his creator, in which the will, intellect, and emotions gratefully respond to the revelation of God's person as expressed in the redemptive work of Christ. This can only occur as the Holy Spirit illuminates God's written Word to a worshiper's mind and heart.

*A quickening of the conscience by the holiness of God, feeding the mind with the truth of God, purging the imagination by the beauty of God, opening the heart to the love of God, and devoting the will to the purpose of God.

The worship service is sometimes compared to a dramatic production with the following participants involved:

The Congregation—the actors whose responsibility is to please the audience—GOD!

The Audience—the Living God.

The Prompters—the various leaders of the service (pastoral staff and musicians), whose responsibilities are to remind the actors of their lines and to ensure that the spotlight remains on the Audience at all times.

Then, the worship service can be thought of as merely the dress rehearsal. The real performance begins when the spiritually rejuvenated believer leaves the sanctuary to begin a new week as God's personal representative in a needy world.

GROUP DISCUSSION
What does the term "worship" mean to you personally? Do you feel spiritually renewed when you leave a worship service, and are you better prepared to face the new week? Why?

SUGGESTED GROUP SINGING
Holy, Holy, Holy, No. 31—*101 Hymn Stories*

THOUGHT
Worship renews the spirit as sleep renews the body.
—Richard Clarke Cabot

THE WORSHIP SERVICE
New Testament Principles

But the hour cometh, and now is, when the true worshipers shall worship the Father in spirit and in truth; for the Father seeketh such to worship Him (John 4:23).

The most complete teaching of the New Testament principles of worship is found in the fourth chapter of John's gospel. Here the Lord confronted a lowly woman from Sychar of Samaria with the all-important issues of life. First He invited her to find the "living water" that alone could provide eternal satisfaction for her longing heart. Then, following the woman's salvation experience, the Lord taught her the meaning of worship. The result was that "many of the Samaritans of that city believed on Him for the saying of the woman, which testified, 'He told me all that I ever did' " (John 4:39). This is always God's pattern for the individual: SALVATION, WORSHIP, and SERVICE.

A startling new concept of worship was introduced to the woman of Samaria. The Lord called for worship "in spirit and in truth"—in personal sincerity and simplicity—a worship no longer based on mere tradition and ritual. Because God is Spirit, He must be worshiped by the corresponding faculty in man. Worship, therefore, is a personal soul expression; it is an attitude of mind and heart rather than a physical or tangible act. In the Old Testament, worship was a mandatory response to God's command. In the New Testament, believers not only worship in obedience to God's unchanging command, but rather because they lovingly desire to fulfill the Father's will. In the Old Testament, man could only approach God through the prescribed rites of the tabernacle or temple. In the New Testament, the Christian individual's relationship with God is immediate and personal. Further, we are instructed that our worship is not limited to a particular place or form, but rather that each believer's body is the temple of God (1 Cor. 6:19, 20). Moreover, the only sacrifices God requires today are the spiritual sacrifices from each believer (Rom. 12:1; Heb. 13:15, 16).

Worship not only should be practiced daily in each believer's devotional life, but as Christians we are commanded to "consider one another to provoke unto love and to good works: not forsaking the assembling of ourselves together, as the manner of some is; but exhorting one another: and so much the more, as ye ye see the day approaching" (Heb. 10:24, 25). Group or corporate worship has the promise of the Lord that "where two or three are gathered together in My name, there am I in the midst of them" (Matt. 18:20).

Let us love our God supremely, let us love each other too;
Let us love and pray for sinners, till our God makes all things new.
Then He'll call us home to heaven, at His table we'll sit down;
Christ will gird Himself and serve us with sweet manna all around. —George Atkins

GROUP DISCUSSION
Why is it important that salvation and worship must always precede our service for God? What benefits can corporate worship provide a believer that worshiping alone cannot?

SUGGESTED GROUP SINGING
All Hail the Power, No. 4—*101 Hymn Stories*
O Worship the King, No. 72—*101 Hymn Stories*

THOUGHT
The Lord's Day is a firm foundation on which to build a six-story week.

Dear Lord, we thank You for the instructions in Your Word and for the Holy Spirit to guide us in our worship. We marvel that You revealed these profound truths to a lowly Samaritan woman rather than to the temple priests, thereby teaching us that You desire the worship of every believer, regardless of his status in life. Help us to worship you in spirit and in truth each time we gather. We ask in Christ's name. Amen.

THE WORSHIP SERVICE
Forms of Worship

I have planted, Apollos watered; but God gave the increase. So then neither is he that planteth anything, neither he that watereth; but God that giveth the increase. For we are laborers together with God (1 Corinthians 3:6, 7, 9).

Because many evangelical churches have no prescribed order of worship, in contrast to the more liturgical churches, the local pastor, board, and music leaders are responsible for preparing a spiritual and effective order of activities for each service. This preparation requires prayerful and thoughtful planning. A service must never degenerate into a traditional routine. A dead ritualism can easily occur, however, even with the simplest orders of service.

Forms or models of worship services vary greatly with different bodies of believers according to their backgrounds, personalities and traditions. Some church leaders feel that true worship is best achieved when it is conducted in a structured, liturgical, and meditative setting. Other sincere believers prefer a freer, often spontaneous, and contemporary approach to worship. A diversity of worship forms is healthy within the evangelical community. The body of Christ must never become divided because of such cultural differences, nor should spirituality be judged by one's personal, subjective preferences. The object of true worship must always be God, not the forms or the personalities involved.

Worship flourishes best in an atmosphere of freedom. "Where the Spirit of the Lord is, there is liberty" (2 Cor. 3:17). Freedom of spirit, however, must not lead to a haphazard, irreverent, or confused service. Freedom is not chaos. The worship of any assembly must assume some outward form. Unity of thought, feeling, and purpose are best achieved through an appropriate structure. The Scriptures teach that all things should be done decently and in order for the purpose of building up one another (1 Cor. 14:26, 33, 40).

Regardless of what form is used, a worship service should be marked by a joyful spirit that is balanced with attitudes of reverence, sincerity, and appropriate behavior. It should be filled with thanksgiving and praise. A meditative atmosphere should enable God's "still small whisper" to be heard. The service should progress so that there is an attitude of eagerness to receive instruction from God's inspired Word. Finally, the service should be challenging—the yielding of the human will to the divine will. A worship service, then, should result in motivating each believer to worthier discipleship and more dynamic crusading for Christ as he returns to his everyday life.

May the mind of Christ, my Savior, live in me from day to day,,

By His love and pow'r controlling all I do and say.

May His beauty rest upon me, as I seek the lost to win,
And may they forget the channel, seeing only Him.

—Kate B. Wilkinson

GROUP DISCUSSION

As a group project, prepare an order of service that you feel would allow the congregation to be more actively and creatively involved in their worship of God. Share an experience that you have had of worshiping with another congregation whose form of worship differed from this church. What was your response?

SUGGESTED GROUP SINGING

How Firm a Foundation, No. 32—*101 Hymn Stories*
There's A Wideness in God's Mercy, No. 89—*101 More Hymn Stories*

THOUGHT

God sends no churches from the skies; out of our hearts they must arise.

THE WORSHIP SERVICE
Revitalizing Worship

Enter into His gates with thanksgiving, and into His courts with praise; be thankful unto Him, and bless His name (Psalm 100:4).

One of the prime functions of a local church is to provide its people with weekly opportunities for meaningful worship. Many evangelical churches today are criticized for the quality of their worship services. These churches are generally effective in evangelism, Christian education, and fellowship, but they are often careless and shallow when it comes to leading a congregation into the presence of God for worship.

Every major spiritual revival in the Old Testament (2 Chron. 7:1-6; 23:18; Ezra 3:10-13; Neh. 12:22-30) and throughout the church-age has led to the revitalizing of praise and worship for God's people. In the past decade, a renewed concern for worship has been experienced by many evangelical leaders. They realize that the congregation must become more actively and creatively involved in worship rather than being mere spectators at a religious performance. Furthermore, the conviction is growing that people need to experience vital personal encounters with God, instead of merely listening to doctrinal treatises, pious platitudes, or some personal manifesto. Only an intimate relationship with the triune God as revealed in the Scriptures can truly satisfy the human heart.

There is no set pattern for the activities of a worship service. The leadership must be earnestly concerned, however, that each activity contributes to the spirit of worship and allows the congregation to hear the voice of the Living God. Worship services will include some form or adaptation of the following elements: expressions of praise and adoration for the triune Godhead, confession of sin, assurance of the acceptance by God, instruction from the Scriptures, and a time for the congregation to commit themselves to the purposes of God.

Some church leaders today, basing their thinking on such

passages as Psalm 100:4, are suggesting that worship services should progress in intensity. Beginning with *thanksgiving,* they should lead to *praise,* and then arrive at *true worship—blessing His Name.*

THANKSGIVING—Expressions of personal gratitude for the daily blessings of life. This first level of worship is compared to the outer court in the Old Testament temple, where worshipers made the initial preparation for their worship—the purchase of animals for sacrifice.

PRAISE—Expressions of gratitude to God for His spiritual provisions. This second level of worship can be compared to the inner court of the Old Testament temple, where the worshipers offered their sacrifices.

WORSHIP: TRUE WORSHIP IS BLESSING GOD'S NAME—Expressions of praise and adoration to God simply for who He is. This third level of worship is compared to the Holy of Holies, where only the High Priest could enter on behalf of the people. With the death of Christ, however, the veil was torn. Since then, every believer-priest has been invited to come boldly into God's presence (Heb. 4:16). The priest, however, had to present himself worthily in the Holy of Holies or be stricken dead. Similarly, there is an appropriate approach to God today. "They that worship Him, must worship Him in spirit and in truth" (John 4:24).

GROUP DISCUSSION
What elements help create a sense of true worship in a service? Which distract?

SUGGESTED GROUP SINGING
Deeper and Deeper, No. 19—*101 Hymn Stories*

THOUGHT
O Lord, grant that I may desire Thee, and desiring Thee, seek Thee, and seeking Thee, find Thee, and finding Thee, be satisfied with Thee forever.   —Augustine

THE RESURRECTION MESSAGE
Lent—A Time of Preparation

For the preaching of the cross is to them that perish foolishness; but unto us which are saved it is the power of God (1 Corinthians 1:18).

Perhaps the most significant event in the life of a local church is the celebration of Easter. On that day we celebrate Christ's triumph over death and the guarantee of immortality His resurrection gives to all who believe in Him. A large segment of Christendom precede this victory celebration with a period of preparation that is much like the time of advent before Christmas. These weeks of Easter preparation are known as the Lenten season. It begins with Ash Wednesday and includes the 40 weekdays and 6 Sundays preceding Easter Sunday. The church color for this season is purple. For many centuries, Christians have used the Lenten season for self-examination and personal discipline in order to enter into the suffering and death of Christ more fully.

For many evangelicals, the term "Lent" conjures up negative feelings. It reminds them of medieval mysticism and superstition. There is the Mardi Gras, the frenzied, carnival-type celebration just before Lent. There is the Ash Wednesday service, when ashes are placed on the foreheads of worshipers as a sign of contrition. These ashes are taken from the burning of the palms used on the previous year's Palm Sunday. Some people strive to deny themselves during Lent, believing that if Christ could suffer for them, they can at least give up some pleasure for Him. Others become very pious and concerned about doing good deeds for their fellowman. These kinds of religious practices are often offensive to evangelical believers and remind them of this warning of the apostle Paul: "Having a form of godliness, but denying the power thereof; from such turn away" (2 Tim. 3:5).

In their reaction to religious practices like these, some evangelicals do not appreciate nor value this season as they should. Christians need to think seriously about the death, burial, and resurrection of Christ. This is the very foundation of the Christian faith, and it cannot be dismissed flippantly. We also need periodic reminders that we are to follow the example of Christ in His concern for the needs of mankind.

Let it be emphasized, however, that service for God and to our fellowman in no way contributes to our personal salvation. Salvation is a free gift from God that we receive by faith (Eph. 2:8, 9). We do good works because they are commanded by Christ and because of our love for Him.

Let us use this Lenten season to deepen our understanding of Christ's suffering and death, and to renew our commitment to serve God and our fellowman. Only the life of faith issuing in deeds of love prepares man, when judged, to stand before God.

O dearly, dearly has He loved, and we must love Him too;
And trust in His redeeming blood, and try His works to do.
—Mrs. Cecil F. Alexander

GROUP DISCUSSION

What concepts does the term "Lent" invoke in your thinking? How can each of us use this season in a positive manner to enrich our spiritual lives?

SUGGESTED GROUP SINGING

In the Cross of Christ I Glory, No. 42—*101 Hymn Stories*

THOUGHT

The only ladder high enough to touch heaven's threshold is the cross of Christ.

Dear God, we give thanks for the salvation You have given us through the suffering and death of Your Son, our Savior. May we use this season to grow in our relationship with You. May Christ's example of concern for the needs of others ever motivate our actions. Help us to truly minister the truths of Thy sacrificial love to our congregation during these special days. We pray in Christ's name. Amen.

THE RESURRECTION MESSAGE
Holy Week—A Time of Contemplation

Let this mind be in you, which was also in Christ Jesus (Philippians 2:5).

The week preceding Easter Sunday is known as Holy or Passion Week. These 7 days have been described as the most intense and important week of history. The dramatic events that occurred during Christ's final days on earth are recorded in all four gospels (Matthew 21; Mark 11; Luke 19; John 12). The very foundations of Christianity and the church rest firmly upon the events of this week:

Palm Sunday: John 12:12-15—The only day of triumph known by Christ in His earthly ministry. A fulfillment of Old Testament prophecy (Zech. 9:9). Christ's lament for the city of Jerusalem (Luke 13:34). The happy "hosannas" which were soon to change to the hysterical cries—"Crucify Him."

The Lord's Holy Anger: 1. At a fig tree that bore no fruit (Matt. 21:18-19). 2. At the moneychangers who were misusing the temple (Matt. 21:12, 13).

The Last Supper: Matthew 26:26-28—Observed on Maundy Thursday, it was instituted by Christ to provide His followers with a lasting memorial of His redemptive death. It would also provide a visible bond with all fellow believers in His Church universal.

The Foot Washing: John 13:4-10—An object lesson taught by Christ regarding the basic qualities of true discipleship: humility, purity, and servanthood.

The Song of Victory: Matthew 26:30—This last song was likely one of the imminent Hallel Psalms, Nos. 115-118. Despite His knowledge of the immediacy of Gethsemane and the death on the cross, Christ faced these events as though already victorious.

Gethsemane: Matthew 26:36-46—Three times Jesus prayed, while His disciples slept, "O My Father, if it be possible, let this cup pass from Me: nevertheless not as I will, but as Thou wilt" (vv. 39, 42, 44).

The Kiss of Betrayal: Mark 14:44; Luke 22:48—"Judas, are you betraying the Son of Man with a kiss?"

The Perverted Trial: Matthew 27:11-26—Christ charged with blasphemy and sentenced to die as a Roman criminal.

The Crucifixion: Matthew 27:33-38—Most Christians believe He was crucified on what is now known as Good Friday. The church color for this day is black. The final words of Christ from the cross:

1. "Father, forgive them; for they know not what they do" (Luke 23:34).

2. "Verily, I say unto thee, today shalt thou be with me in paradise" (Luke 23:43).

3. "Woman, behold thy son! Behold thy mother" (John 19:26, 27).

4. "My God, My God, why hast Thou forsaken Me?" (Matthew 27:46).

5. "I thirst" (John 19:28).

6. "It is finished!" (John 19:30).

7. "Father, into Thy hands I commend My spirit" (Luke 23:46).

GROUP DISCUSSION

Choose one event of Holy Week and tell what it means to you personally.

SUGGESTED GROUP SINGING

O Sacred Head, Now Wounded, No. 70—*101 More Hymn Stories*

THOUGHT

Jesus cannot forget us; we have been engraven on the palms of His hands.   —Lois Picillo

THE RESURRECTION MESSAGE
Easter—A Time of Celebration

And if Christ be not risen, then is our preaching vain, and your faith is also vain (1 Corinthians 15:14).

The capstone of the Christian faith is the resurrection of Jesus Christ. It is the completion of our salvation:

For if, when we were enemies, we were reconciled to God by the death of His Son, much more, being reconciled, we shall be saved by His life (Rom. 5:10).

The validity of the gospel message rests on the fact that Jesus is alive. Many evidences for the literal resurrection of Christ could be given, including His post-resurrection encounters with the disciples and His appearance to more than 500 eyewitnesses at one time. Even so, the most convincing evidence still stems from a transformed life of one who can say with conviction, "He lives within my heart!"

Easter Sunday is the beginning of a new season in the church year known as Eastertide. It begins with Easter Sunday and extends for 50 days, concluding with Pentecost Sunday—the advent of the Holy Spirit. The church color for this season is white. The period also includes another important observance, Ascension Day, 40 days after Easter.

The message of the empty tomb is the very heartbeat of Christian worship. Consider the changes that began with the resurrection:

*With the resurrection came a new day for worship—the first day of the week rather than the traditional Sabbath worship. In one sense, every Sunday should be an Easter celebration.

*With the resurrection came the defeat of man's ultimate enemy—death (1 Cor. 15:55, 57).

*With the resurrection came the promise of immortality. "Because I live, ye shall live also" (John 14:19).

In the resurrection account, the angel gave two commands that apply as much to us today as they did to the seeking women (Matthew 28:6, 7):

*"Come, see the place"—Christ's resurrection demands a personal encounter.

*"Go, quickly, and tell"—Christ's resurrection must be shared with others.

Music can be a powerful pronouncement of the resurrection message. When the thrilling pageantry of Easter is wedded to worthy music, the resurrection becomes an unforgettable reality. May choir and congregation truly celebrate Christ's victory this Easter!

> Arise, O soul, this Easter Day!
> Forget the tomb of yesterday,
> For thou from bondage art set free;
> Thou sharest in His victory
> And life eternal is for thee,
> Because the Lord is risen. —Unknown

GROUP DISCUSSION

Speculate about how you would have felt if you had been a believer on that first Easter morning. How is the resurrection the completion of our salvation?

SUGGESTED GROUP SINGING

Christ the Lord Is Risen Today, No. 13—*101 Hymn Stories*
He Lives, No. 33—*101 More Hymn Stories*

THOUGHT

The resurrection is a fact of history without which history does not make sense. —C.H. Pinnock

Heavenly Father, we rejoice as we think of the empty tomb. We are glad for a risen, ascended Savior, who sits at Your right hand to intercede for us. Fill us, Lord, with the power of the resurrection as we seek to live and serve for Your glory. We pray in Christ's name. Amen.

THE RESURRECTION MESSAGE
The Emmaus Road—A Time of Dedication

Did not our hearts burn within us, while He talked with us by the way, and while He opened to us the Scriptures (Luke 24:32)?

The Emmaus account is always thrilling to read and ponder. Retrace with Cleopas and his wife Mary, whom many believe to be the two Emmaus disciples, on that first resurrection day, the wearisome seven-mile journey from Jerusalem to their village of Emmaus. Very likely, only three days earlier this couple had witnessed the cruel death of the One they earnestly believed would be the redeemer of Israel (John 19:25). This morning further disturbing news had come by some of Jesus' followers: His body was no longer in the tomb. The most feasible explanation for this startling turn of events was that the women who had gone to the tomb early that morning had seen a vision. Now it was necessary for the pair to return to their home in Emmaus before nightfall. While busily discussing the hectic events of the past three days, they were suddenly joined by a stranger, who immediately entered into their conversation. The stranger began to explain directly from the Scriptures the meaning of the events they had witnessed. It wasn't until the couple reached their home and invited their guest to stay and share a meal with them that "their eyes were opened, and they knew Him." This personal encounter produced within them "burning hearts." Forgetting their fatigue, Cleopas and Mary returned to Jerusalem that same hour to share their joyous experience with the other disciples.

In a real sense, everyone who would be an effective representative for Christ needs an Emmaus Road experience. There must be the transformation of life from disbelief and discouragement to that of the "burning heart," the intense desire to share the good news with others. Reaffirming the resurrection message should result in resurrection power, joy, and true devotion—the afterglow of Easter.

One of the realities of the Christian life, however, is the difficulty of consistently maintaining spiritual warmth. Our relationship with God and our service for Him can often be compared to a roller coaster, a series of highs and lows. Pastors and church leaders know too well the meaning of the post-Easter slump—and choirs are no exception.

How, then, does a believer maintain the Easter afterglow? Certainly there will be the days of discouragements and problems. Yet for the Christian, each day must become a new adventure of faith as well as a rededication of oneself to His glory. The Scriptures must be the sourcebook for answers to life's perplexing problems. Each day requires a fresh appropriation of Scriptural promises such as these:

"When thou passest through the waters, I will be with thee" (Isaiah 43:2).
"Cast thy burden upon the Lord, and He shall sustain thee" (Psalm 55:22).

Yes, life is like the Emmaus road, and we tread it not alone,
For beside us walks the Son of God, to uphold and keep His own.
And our hearts within us thrill with joy at His words of love and grace,
And the blessed hope that when day is done we shall see His blessed face.   —Avis B. Christiansen

GROUP DISCUSSION

What suggestions can you offer for maintaining the Easter afterglow in an individual's life as well as in the life of this church? In the ministry of this choir?

SUGGESTED GROUP SINGING

Because He Lives, No. 11—*101 More Hymn Stories*

THOUGHT

The antidote for occupation burn-out is a "burning heart" for God.

THE CREATIVE SPIRIT
New Awareness and New Appreciations

Behold, I make all things new (Revelation 21:5).

An essential element of the Christian faith is "newness." This creative quality is consistent with the nature of God. "In the beginning God created..." (Gen. 1:1). "If any man be in Christ, he is a new creation..." (2 Cor. 5:7).

Man is the crowning glory of God's creative acts, and God and man share creativity as an integral part of their being. God created the world *ex nihilo,* out of nothing. Man, in turn, imitates God by using the materials of nature to create new things. God created the trees; man is able to build functional furniture and fashion artistic wooden carvings. God created the laws of sound; man is able to compose and perform music.

God has endowed man with five wonderful senses: hearing, sight, touch, smell, and taste. Developing these senses enables us to receive and experience countless impulses and inspiration each day. These in turn motivate our lives with new appreciations, thus keeping us from monotony and stagnation.

Often the little things of life and nature provide us with these new appreciations. Sometimes it is an awareness of an unusual sunset or cloud formation, the sound of a particular voice, the delicate taste of food, a fragrant aroma, or the touch of a hand. Any of these can stimulate the imagination of an individual whose God-given sensory perceptions are alive. In addition, we can develop an awareness of and appreciation for the artistic expressions of our fellowmen. The creative spirit is the beginning of a lifetime of real enjoyment.

The Scriptures contain numerous references to man's five perceptual senses:

Hearing—Isa. 55:3; Mark 4:24-25; Luke 8:18; Rev. 2:7.

Sight—Deut. 34:4; Isa. 32:3; Mark 8:18.

Touch—Zech. 2:8; Jer. 1:19; Matt. 9:21; Mark 10:13.

Smell—Psa. 115:6; John 39:25; Eph. 5:2; Phil. 4:18.

Taste—Psa. 34:8; Psa. 119:103: 1 Peter 2:3.

As image-bearers of a creative God, believers have been endowed with distinctive gifts that God wants us to use in reflection of His creative attribute. Sharing one's creativity and talents can be a source of encouragement and edification for our fellow-believers. It can also become a demonstration of spiritual reality to non-Christians. Any believer who does not enjoy and use his creative gifts is forfeiting much of the abundant life promised him by God. And someday each of us will be required to give an accounting of the stewardship of His gifts.

When all Thy mercies, O my God, my rising soul surveys,
Transported with the view, I'm lost in wonder, love, and
praise.   —Joseph Addison

GROUP DISCUSSION

How can this church encourage a greater spirit of creativity in the lives of our people, both young and old? Perhaps special months could be designated for:

The encouragement of original writing—articles, stories, poetry.

The encouragement of original visual works—paintings, church banners, sculpture, photography.

The encouragement of original sacred songs and choruses.

The encouragement of original handicraft.

SUGGESTED GROUP SINGING

This Is My Father's World, No. 97—*101 Hymn Stories*

THOUGHT

It is not how much we have, but how much we enjoy, that makes happiness.   —Charles Haddon Spurgeon

THE CREATIVE SPIRIT
A New Awareness and Appreciation of Family

Lo, children are an heritage from the Lord (Psalm 127:3).

Even though God deals with us as individuals, He has delegated authority to three important institutions for our good: THE FAMILY, THE CHURCH, and THE STATE. Each of these agencies has God-given responsibilities to fulfill.

The Family. As the basic unit of society, the family is the first social group of history. Its purposes are twofold: (1) to beget children, and (2) as a moral training ground. It is here that children learn how to incorporate their individuality into a higher unity. All true family life stems from God (Eph. 3:15).

The Church. As the pillar and ground of the truth (1 Tim. 3:15), the church is the supernatural entity where believers are to grow in faith and in preparation for the life to come. It does so through proclamation, prayer, praise, fellowship, and the ordinances.

The State. As the protector of basic rights and freedoms, the state is the divinely ordained institution for maintaining justice (Rom. 13:1). Its leaders are accountable to God (Col. 1:16) for approving good and punishing evil.

Every believer, in turn, has a responsibility to these three agencies. In the area of the family, the Scriptures are explicit regarding the relationship that should exist between husband and wife and between parents and children. Note these biblical imperatives:

"Honor your father and your mother" (Exod. 20:12).

"Husbands, love your wives..." (Eph. 5:22).

"Wives, submit to your husbands as unto the Lord" (Eph. 5:22).

"Fathers, do not exasperate your children" (Eph. 6:4).

One of the joys of a family relationship is its improvement with time. The years a husband and wife share should deepen the bonds of love, concern, and trust. And many parents have experienced the joy of having their children become their closest and dearest friends. This is much like our Lord's maturing relationship with His disciples: "Henceforth I call you not servants ... but I have called you friends" (John 15:15).

During this season when we celebrate Mother's Day, Father's Day, and Children's Day, let us pray for a new appreciation of God's gift of family.

Happy the home when God is there, and love fills ev'ry breast;
When one their wish and one their prayer and one their heav'nly rest.   —Henry Ware

GROUP DISCUSSION

What can this church do to promote stronger family loyalties and relationships? Share suggestions for improving the spiritual atmosphere of our homes—creative family devotions, group activities, musical recordings, positive use of television ...

SUGGESTED GROUP SINGING

I Would Be True, No. 43—*101 More Hymn Stories*

THOUGHT

The church universal is God's family. It should be seen in miniature in each Christian home.

Dear Heavenly Father, we praise Thee we've been chosen, adopted, accepted in the beloved, in the Christian family. Show me where I need to bring new life into my family relationships. Help me to realize with conviction the priority of responsibility that I have for each member of my family. May the love and concern that you have for those in Your family be my daily model. Help us to realize that neither our church nor our country will ever be what they should be for You without strong Christian homes. In the name of Christ. Amen.

THE CREATIVE SPIRIT

A New Awareness and Appreciation of Pentecost

And when the day of Pentecost was fully come, they were all with one accord in one place ... and they were all filled with the Holy Spirit (Acts 2:1-4).

Another of the important days in the life of any church is Pentecost Sunday—the celebration of the Holy Spirit's advent. This event occurs 50 days or 7 Sundays after Easter. The church color for Pentecost is red. The following Sunday is Trinity Sunday, when we honor each Person of the triune Godhead.

It is essential that we worship the Father as the Eternal God and vital that we worship the Son as our personal Redeemer; but it is equally important that we worship the indwelling Holy Spirit as our Illuminator. Without the ministry of the Holy Spirit, our understanding and appreciation of the Father and Son would be incomplete. Note briefly these 10 specific ministries of the Holy Spirit:

*Teaches truths about God and reveals Christ (1 Cor. 2:10, 11; John 16:12-15).

*Convicts of sin, righteousness and judgment (John 16:8-11).

*Regenerates and renews (Titus 3:5).

*Baptizes/places us into the Body of Christ (1 Cor. 12:13).

*Gives assurance of salvation (Rom. 8:16).

*Indwells and guides our lives (1 Cor. 6:19, 20; Rom. 8:14).

*Prays for us (Rom. 8:26).

*Fills our lives with joy and power (Eph. 5:18).

*Seals/guarantees our eternal promise (Eph. 4:30).

*Distributes gifts to the church (1 Cor. 12:3).

In recent years, a new awareness and an appreciation of the Holy Spirit's ministries have arisen within the church. This concern, known by many as the charismatic or Pentecostal movement, has had a profound influence among many church groups. It should be noted that not all Christians accept completely the teachings and practices of this movement; even so, this new reminder of the presence and power of the Holy Spirit was much needed. All Christians should agree that every believer needs a continuing awareness of the Holy Spirit's presence and the daily appropriation of His power for victorious, fruitful living and effective spiritual service.

May we not become so engrossed with our theological differences about the Holy Spirit that we forfeit the practical benefits of living and walking in the Spirit and demonstrating to a lost world the fruit of a Spirit-filled life. Let us lead our congregation on this Pentecost Sunday into a new awareness and appreciation of the Holy Spirit—the co-existent and co-equal third Person of the Godhead.

Breathe on me, Breath of God, fill me with life anew;
That I may love what Thou dost love, and do what Thou
    wouldst do.   —Edwin Hatch

GROUP DISCUSSION

Discuss this statement: "The Holy Spirit is the most neglected and least understood Person of the Godhead." What can this church do to bring more attention to the importance of the Holy Spirit and His specific ministries?

SUGGESTED GROUP SINGING

Spirit of God, Descend Upon My Heart, No. 84—*101 Hymn Stories*

Holy Ghost, with Light Divine, No. 37—*101 More Hymn Stories*

THOUGHT

Sin, in the case of the unredeemed, is a transgression of the law (Rom. 4:15); in the case of the redeemed, it is the neglecting or the wounding of the Holy Spirit (Eph. 4:30).

THE CREATIVE SPIRIT

A New Awareness and Appreciation of Country

Render therefore unto Caesar the things which are Caesar's; and unto God the things that are God's (Matthew 22:21).

Another important institution ordained by God for the good of man is that of government or the state. Without the rule of good government, man would live in chaos. We can be grateful for good laws and their enforcement. We can be thankful for police and fire protection, for the privilege of voting, and for the right of free speech. In all the world, in no country do the people have more freedom than in the United States of America. Above all, we can be thankful that we are free to gather in groups to worship God and to sing whatever hymns and songs we choose.

God raised up government for our good. As Christian citizens, we are to obey all laws of the land (except those that force us to disobey a direct command of God). We are to pray for our rulers, that peace may prevail so that we can be free to fulfill our divinely ordained purpose of doing the work of the church and sending forth the message of Christ (Rom. 13:1-7).

In addition, we would do well to remember those who have given their lives to keep us free. In love of country, and in many instances in loyalty to God, heroic men and women of the past have laid down their lives to keep us free—and this includes the freedom to worship as we please.

As we celebrate in America another national holiday, especially remembering those who died for the preservation of this land, let us also give thanks to God for the institution of government. May we pray daily for those who have rule over us, both nationally and locally. May we exercise our Christian responsibility to be "lights" and "salt" in our society, ever witnessing to the truth that "righteousness exalteth a nation, but sin is a reproach to any people" (Prov. 14:34).

And may we not be found among those who despise our

leaders or who speak poorly of this great nation. Rather, let us be living demonstrations of the meaning of the motto that appears on our coins, "IN GOD WE TRUST."

Our fathers' God, to Thee, author of liberty, to Thee we sing:
Long may our land be bright with freedom's holy light;
Protect us by Thy might, Great God, our King!
—Samuel Frances Smith

GROUP DISCUSSION

How active a role do you feel a Christian should take in the affairs of government both nationally and locally? Can you give specific instances when it would be proper for a Christian to disobey a law of the land?

SUGGESTED GROUP SINGING

The Star-Spangled Banner, No. 94—*101 Hymn Stories*
America The Beautiful, No. 7—101 More Hymn Stories
God of Our Fathers, No. 28—*101 More Hymn Stories*

THOUGHT

Whatever makes men good Christians makes them good citizens.   —Daniel Webster

The price of liberty is eternal vigilance.

Our Heavenly Father, author of liberty, we thank You for every freedom we have to enjoy. We are most thankful for the freedom to worship as we please. We remember with humble gratitude all those of the past who gave their lives that we might be free today. Give to us that same spirit of sacrifice and a prayerful concern for good government that these freedoms may be preserved for future generations. We pray in Christ's name. Amen.

EFFECTIVE SINGING—
EFFECTIVE SERVICE

Round, clear tones—Full, pure lives

Search me, O God, and know my heart; try me, and know my thoughts; and see if there be any wicked way in me, and lead me in the way everlasting (Psalm 139:23, 24).

A number of parallels can be made between singing well and serving God effectively. The following descriptions are characteristics of a good singing tone:

1. A quality of roundness, richness, and pleasantness of sound.

2. A feeling of flow and ease.

3. A quality of clearness and naturalness.

Singers must realize that one of the chief prerequisites for achieving these qualities is breathing deeply. The air stream is the vehicle that carries and maintains a singer's melodious and resonant sounds. Strain and harshness should never be present in a well-trained voice. Good breathing is possible when a singer develops an upright, confident posture—not allowing himself to become slouchy and careless.

A good vocalist will also sing with clarity. A good tone will be pure—not affected or distorted. When singers produce clear vowel sounds and distinct consonants for each word, listeners will understand the song's message.

By comparison, the flow of breath does for our singing what communion, prayer, and familiarity with the Scriptures do for our walk with God. A devotional life is as basic to our spiritual lives as breathing is to our natural lives. There will be no depth of spirituality nor effective service, until an intimate relationship with the Lord is established on a daily, continual basis. What the spine does for good vocal breathing, the bowed knee and the humble spirit do for our spiritual welfare.

The believer's personal lifestyle, too, must be one of purity, sincerity, and transparent honesty. What people see and hear must be "what they get." There is no place in God's service for deception of any kind. The name that we bear, the songs that we sing, and the life that we live must always be consistent. When these qualities are evident in our lives, unbelievers will begin to hear and understand the gospel message.

I want a principle within of watchful, godly fear,
A sensibility of sin, a pain to feel it near.
Help me the first approach to feel of pride or wrong desire,
To catch the wand'ring of my will and quench the kindling
fire.   —Charles Wesley

GROUP DISCUSSION

What particular tonal quality do you most enjoy and appreciate in other singers? Can you make a parallel comparison between this vocal quality and a particular spiritual virtue in a believer's life?

SUGGESTED GROUP SINGING

Cleanse Me, No. 16—*101 More Hymn Stories*
O For a Closer Walk With God, No. 67—*101 More Hymn Stories*

THOUGHT

A Christian who truly prays as he should will soon endeavor to live as he prays.

Dear Lord, help us to serve You effectively with our voices as well as with our lives. May the richness of our tones reflect the depth of our spiritual living. May the integrity of the gospel message never become distorted and misunderstood by unbelievers because of our disobedient or shallow living. Help us to know ourselves as You know us. May we be willing to pray with the psalmist: "Search me, O God, and know my heart." In the name of our victorious Savior, we pray. Amen.

EFFECTIVE SINGING—
EFFECTIVE SERVICE

Rhythmic Vitality—Spiritual Dynamic

For the kingdom of God is not food and drink, but righteousness, and peace, and joy in the Holy Spirit. For he that in these things serveth Christ is acceptable to God, and approved of men (Romans 14:17, 18).

Another of the parallels that can be made between singing well and serving God effectively is the need for dynamic vitality.

Rhythm is the foundation of music. Although the other basic elements of music—melody, harmony, and form—must be present to make music complete, rhythm is the only element that can exist independently.

Every song needs to be rhythmically alive. It must be characterized by a steady underlying pulsation. Music must always give evidence of movement and flow; it must be going somewhere. A sluggish, irregular rhythm will make any song irritating rather than enjoyable to the listener.

The believer's life and service must also give evidence of aliveness, dynamicness, and a sensitivity to the Holy Spirit's leading. It is quite possible for Christians to have enough faith to assure them of heaven but not enough to make them dynamic in their daily living. What rhythm does for music, the Holy Spirit does in a believer's life. A Spirit-filled person shows that he has a purpose for living, as the Apostle Paul testified, "For me, living is Christ ..." (Phil. 1:21). There is no time or place for an attitude of lethargy in a Spirit-filled life, for this person realizes the brevity of life and desires to make every day count for Christ.

The motto of the Olympian athletes could well be adopted by believers who want to be effective representatives for God: FASTER, HIGHER, and STRONGER. Yet all striving in our own strength is ultimately doomed to failure. We must have the daily energizing of the Holy Spirit's power. E. Paul Hovey has stated:

> The word 'comforter' as applied to the Holy Spirit needs to be translated by some more vigorous term. Literally, it means 'with strength.' Jesus promised His followers that 'the strengthener' would be with them forever. This promise is no lullaby for the faint-hearted. It is a blood transfusion for courageous living.

> Joys are flowing like a river since the Comforter has come;
> He abides with us forever, makes the trusting heart His home.

> Blessed quietness, holy quietness, what assurance in my soul!
> On the stormy sea He speaks peace to me, how the billows
> cease to roll!   —Manie P. Ferguson

GROUP DISCUSSION

It has been said that motivation may get us started, but a good habit keeps us going. Discuss the spiritual habits that you have found most helpful in your own life. What is your response when someone in the church comments, "I've had my day, now let someone else do this task"?

SUGGESTED GROUP SINGING

Lead On, O King Eternal, No. 54—*101 Hymn Stories*
Be Thou My Vision, No. 10—*101 More Hymn Stories*

THOUGHT

A little faith will bring your soul to heaven, but much faith will bring heaven to your soul.   —D.L. Moody

Dear Lord, we confess that we often become lethargic in Your service. We so easily lose the thrill and dynamic that once we knew. We realize that this wrong attitude develops when we try to live and serve in our own strength. May we allow Your Holy Spirit to rejuvenate our individual lives, as well as that of our church, giving us that inward strength and leadership that assure our ministry for You may again be all You intend it to be. In Christ's name, Amen.

EFFECTIVE SINGING—
EFFECTIVE SERVICE
Interpretation and Communication—
Witnessing and Sharing

Let your light so shine before men, that they may see your good works, and glorify your Father, who is in heaven (Matthew 5:16).

The ultimate goal of good singing is the communication of a message. Though fine tones and rhythmic verve are necessary, they are not ends in themselves. Singers must never be content with merely making it through a song, or even achieving lovely sounds and good diction with rhythmic precision. Rather, a singer must earnestly desire that his song make a spiritual impact upon each hearer.

For one to interpret and communicate a song effectively, the following conditions should be true. Each singer must:

1. Understand thoroughly the text he is singing. He should be able to express in his own words the meaning and emotional connotations of all the words in the song.

2. Believe what he is singing. The interpretation must be based on absolute conviction and sincerity.

3. Become completely absorbed in what he is singing. He cannot lose concentration if he is to communicate effectively.

4. Identify the most important words in a phrase and know where the proper stress and accents should be placed.

5. Be so involved in the music that he is able to visualize the meaning and emotional implications of the song. Only in this way will facial expressions and gestures be natural and appropriate for the occasion.

The ultimate goal of singing and the principles involved in achieving that goal parallel the purpose for Christian living and service. Though it is wonderful to know God and to enjoy

His daily fellowship, one reason for His choosing us was that we might represent Him and share His message with others. To do that effectively, we must have a clear understanding of that message as recorded in the Scriptures. It is always important to stress the major truths when witnessing, and not to become involved in secondary or divisive issues. A believer's life also must reflect the absolute conviction that a personal relationship with God is a priority for every individual, and that no life is complete, until that person is on intimate terms with his Creator and Redeemer. Above all, effective service for God requires a life that is completely absorbed with Him. Thinking about God and relating to Him must be more than a Sunday experience. Regardless of our life's vocation, the pursuit of God and His glory must become our total and natural way of living.

In a small cemetery was found this anonymous epitaph: "Here lies the body of John Smith, who for 40 years cobbled shoes in this village to the glory of God."

"So whether you eat, or drink, or whatever you do, do it all for the glory of God" (1 Cor. 10:31).

GROUP DISCUSSION

Discuss specific suggestions that each person can put into practice for being more effective in sharing God's message and promoting His glory on the job, in the home, and among one's friends.

SUGGESTED GROUP SINGING

Rescue the Perishing, No. 76—*101 Hymn Stories*
Let the Lower Lights Be Burning, No. 55—*101 More Hymn Stories*

THOUGHT

I will place no value on anything I have or may possess except in relation to the Kingdom of Christ.   —David Livingstone

EFFECTIVE SINGING—
EFFECTIVE SERVICE
Vocal Blend—Christian Unity

By this shall all men know that ye are My disciples, if ye have love one to another (John 13:35).

Effective choral singing depends on a group's blend. Though fine individual voices are an asset to any choir, singers must learn the art of producing a unified sound. There is no place in a church choir for a "prima donna" attitude.

I was impressed again with this recently while watching a professional choir rehearse. The main concern of each singer was that of listening intently to the voices next to him. The vocalists continually tilted their heads toward their fellow singers and consciously tried to match and imitate the tonal quality of their neighbors. Where there was a melodic move-ment in one voice line, the other parts responded with awareness and support. The final result was breathtaking. There is no more lovely sound in music than the sound of well-blended voices.

In a similar manner, God's representatives must work hard to present a unified message to this lost generation. In the Christian ministry there is no place for the haughty spirit, either by individuals or by groups. We all need each other. Part of spiritual maturity is learning to love, accept, and appreciate our brothers and sisters in the family of God.

An adult church choir should be characterized by a spirit of genuine camaraderie. Unfriendly or jealous attitudes should never appear. Little cliques must never form within the choir. This group should be the most closely knit organization within the entire church.

Oh, for a spirit of oneness among all true believers. Fidelity to Christ—who prayed for all Christians to be one so that the world would believe—requires that Christians pursue the cause of unity (John 17:21). To allow ourselves to become fragmented over minor doctrinal interpretations or differences in methodology only distorts the pure sounds of the gospel.

Let us resolve to be even more effective in the choir ministry of this local church in the days ahead. Let us also determine to live with spiritual depth and fullness, purity and transparency. May our lives communicate the good news with conviction. But in so doing, may we always take time to love and appreciate our fellow family members in God's church universal.

Wherever men adore Thee, our souls with them would kneel;
Wherever men implore Thy help, their trouble we would feel;
And where men do Thy service, though knowing not Thy sign,
Our hand is with them in good work, for they are also Thine.
—Henry van Dyke

GROUP DISCUSSION

What suggestions can you offer for improving the vocal as well as the spiritual blend of this choir? What suggestions can you offer for this church to present a more unified spiritual voice to this community?

SUGGESTED GROUP SINGING

Blest Be the Tie That Binds, No. 12—*101 Hymn Stories*

THOUGHT

There is no leveler like Christianity, but it levels by lifting all who receive it to the lofty table-land of a true character and of undying hope both for this world and the next.
—Jonathan Edwards

We thank You, Heavenly Father, for the privilege we have had this past year to represent You in our choir ministry and as individuals. Give us the desire and strength to be more effective in the days ahead. Help us to have a greater love for one another. Keep us from developing a selfish, provincial spirit. May we earnestly seek to blend our lives and talents with true believers everywhere in the furtherance of Thy kingdom. In the name of Christ, our Lord, Amen.

REFORMATION SUNDAY

God is our refuge and strength, a very present help in trouble (Psalm 46:1).

One of the most important days in Protestant church history is October 31, 1517. This was the date on which an Augustinian monk named Martin Luther made his way to the doors of the Cathedral of Wittenberg, Germany, and posted his famous 95 theses (complaints) against the teachings and practices of the Roman church. A short time later, those who withstood the papal ultimatum to refute Luther's teachings were first called "protestants." From the Protestant Reformation movement, three important developments arose which have become basic tenets of evangelical Protestantism to the present time:

*The reestablishment of the Scriptures as sole and ultimate authority for Christians—not the decrees of the church leaders.

*The clarifying of the means of salvation. Individuals are made right with God through a personal response of faith to Christ's finished work—"justification by faith alone"—and not through the seven sacraments of the church or by one's good works.

*The restoration of congregational singing. Congregational singing had been halted since the close of the fourth century, when the church leaders decreed: "If laymen are not to interpret the Scriptures for themselves, so they are not to sing the songs of the church." Martin Luther declared, "Let God speak directly to His people through the Scriptures, and let His people respond with grateful songs of praise."

Interestingly, the vehicle God used to fan these Reformation teachings was a hymn by Martin Luther, "A Mighty Fortress Is Our God," based on Psalm 46. Luther's enemies often lamented that "the German people were singing themselves into Luther's doctrines, and that his hymns destroyed more souls than all of his writings and sermons." From that time to the present, congregational singing has been one of the most important activities in evangelical church worship. With this awareness and conviction, choir members should always strive to be good leaders of enthusiastic, vibrant congregational singing.

Although Martin Luther was most noted as a theologian and not a musician, he is credited with writing 36 hymns and with composing the music for many of his own texts. He was also known for his fine tenor voice, as well as his mastery of the flute and the lute. Luther had a high regard for the ministry of music, for he wrote:

> There is a root-like unity of music and theology. Music is wrapped and locked in theology.

> I would allow no man to preach or teach God's people who did not realize the power and use of sacred music.

Many church historians today state that more converts were won to faith in Christ through Luther's encouragement of congregational singing than were influenced by his strong preaching and teaching.

> Let goods and kindred go, this mortal life also;
> The body they may kill: God's truth abideth still—
> His kingdom is forever.   —Martin Luther

GROUP DISCUSSION

Why are the three major emphases that were an outgrowth of the 16th-century Protestant Reformation movement so important in our church life today? What reforms do you feel are needed today to make 20th-century, evangelical Protestantism more relevant in these times?

SUGGESTED GROUP SINGING

A Mighty Fortress Is Our God, No. 1—*101 Hymn Stories*

THOUGHT

The Devil, the originator of sorrowful anxieties and restless troubles, flees before the sound of music almost as much as before the Word of God.   —Martin Luther

ADVENT

Unto you that fear My name shall the Sun of Righteousness arise with healing in His wings (Malachi 4:2).

The advent season begins on the fourth Sunday before Christmas Eve. The emphasis centers on the Old Testament prophecies concerning a coming Messiah and His establishment of an earthly kingdom. The traditional church color for this season is purple, symbolic of the promised Messiah's royalty. Many churches observe this time by lighting a new candle each Sunday preceding Christmas.

The Messiah was first prophesied in the 6th century B.C., when the Jews were taken captive in Babylon. For centuries thereafter, faithful Hebrews looked for their promised Redeemer with great longing and expectation, echoing the prayer that He would ransom captive Israel.

Perhaps the most bleak period in Israel's history was the intertestamental period, the 400 silent years between the close of the Book of Malachi and the Gospel of Matthew. The Jewish hope of a Messiah was all but lost in times of extreme cruelty and destruction from the hands of such enemies as the Egyptians, Syrians, and Romans. Finally the long-awaited heavenly announcement came:

For unto you is born this day in the city of David a Savior, which is Christ the Lord (Luke 2:11).

The tragedy of tragedies is the biblical and historical truth that the Messiah came to His own people to establish a spiritual kingdom of both redeemed Jews and Gentiles, but that His own rejected Him. The good news is that citizenship in God's kingdom became available to all who respond with personal faith to the redemptive work of God's Son, the Messiah-Savior (John 1:11, 12).

Anticipation is a necessary and important part of every believer's life. In Old Testament days the people awaited a

Messianic kingdom. New Testament believers have been further instructed that hope is one of the three important and abiding ingredients in life: faith, hope, and love (1 Cor. 13:13).

Faith initiates the believer's relationship with God, hope maintains its vitality, and love, the greatest of the three, is its supreme demonstration. The ultimate hope for believers today is the anticipation of the sound of the trumpet announcing the second advent of our Lord and the beginning of His eternal reign as King of Kings and Lord of Lords!

> Come, Thou long-expected Jesus, born to set Thy people free;
> From our fears and sins release us: let us find our rest in Thee.
> Israel's Strength and Consolation, hope of all the earth Thou art;
> Dear Desire of ev'ry nation, joy of ev'ry longing heart.
>
> —Charles Wesley

GROUP DISCUSSION

What parallels are there between the problems many people seem to have in accepting Christ as their Savior and the difficulties the Jewish people have had in accepting Christ as their promised Messiah? How can we best reach people, Jew or Gentile, who are sincerely searching for the truth? How does a knowledge of the Old Testament prophetic details about Christ's birth strengthen the believer's anticipation of the promised second advent?

SUGGESTED GROUP SINGING

O Come, O Come, Emmanuel, No. 64—*101 Hymn Stories*

THOUGHT

How proper it is that Christians should follow advent. For Him who looks toward the future, the manger is situated on Golgotha, and the cross has already been raised in Bethlehem.

> —Dag Hammarskjöld

EPIPHANY

And when they were come into the house, they (the wise men) saw the young child with Mary His mother, and fell down, and worshiped Him; and when they had opened their treasures, they presented unto Him gifts; gold, and frankincense, and myrrh (Matthew 2:11).

The period in the church year that begins with January 6 and extends to Ash Wednesday, or the Wednesday before the sixth Sunday preceding Easter, is known as Epiphany. The church color throughout this season is green.

The emphasis of Epiphany is that of the Christ Child being revealed to the wise men as His first manifestation to the Gentiles as the light of the world. It is generally believed that these wise men from the East arrived approximately two years after the birth of Christ. In many churches, Epiphany is ushered in with a special week of prayer, a renewed commitment to evangelism, and a worldwide concern for missions. As an aftermath of Christmas, it is a time when the early events of Christ's life are often taught (Luke 2:52).

The gifts presented to the Christ Child by the wise men after their long search were both significant and appropriate: gold, symbolic of His kingly reign; frankincense, symbolic of His priestly ministry; myrrh, symbolic of our redemption through His death. How important it is that our gifts of love and devotion be offered to Christ after we have first found Him and have bowed in true adoration before Him.

Epiphany should also be a reminder to each of us that God wants His message heard beyond the four walls of the church. May we use this time to sharpen our vision and perfect our strategy for reaching lost individuals in our community and world. Perhaps during this season the choir could engage in some special outreach projects such as singing in a shopping center, jail service, juvenile hall, hospital, nursing home, or military base. As individual believers, may we be reminded and challenged to share God's love both by word and deed with those He brings into our lives. May the truth of John 20:21 ever motivate our witness:

"As My Father hath sent Me, even so send I you."

As with gladness men of old did the guiding star behold;
And with joy they hailed its light, leading onward, beaming bright;
So most gracious God, may we evermore be led to Thee

As with joyful steps they sped to that lowly manger bed;
There to bend the knee before Him whom heav'n and earth adore;
So may we with willing feet ever seek the mercy seat.

—William C. Dix

GROUP DISCUSSION

How can an awareness of the prophecies of the advent season, the celebration of Christmas, and an understanding of the meaning of Epiphany deepen our appreciation of Christ's coming into this world? What specific projects could the choir pursue during this Epiphany season to bring the gospel message to those outside of this church? Share an interesting experience that you have had recently in discussing the claims of Christ with a non-Christian.

SUGGESTED GROUP SINGING

In Christ There Is No East or West, No. 41—*101 Hymn Stories*
So Send I You, No. 82—*101 Hymn Stories*

THOUGHT

Christ is not valued at all unless He be valued above all.

—Augustine

OTHER HELPFUL BOOKS
By Kenneth W. Osbeck

SINGING WITH UNDERSTANDING
Study the historical growth of hymnody, note the seven specific suggestions for the use of music in worship. Includes 101 favorite hymn backgrounds. 336 pp.

101 HYMN STORIES
Excellent for devotional reading, sermon illustrations, bulletin inserts of historical information. Includes actual music for each hymn. 288 pp.

101 "MORE" HYMN STORIES
Stories that inspired the hymn writers, including some from the 20th century with its variety of hymn styles, will enhance your worship. 328 pp.

MINISTRY OF MUSIC
Covers all phases of sacred music, history, spiritual concepts, an analysis of trends, practical suggestions for various age groups. 192 pp.

POCKET GUIDE FOR THE CHURCH CHOIR MEMBER
Basic music review, suggestions to improve your ability to read music, vocal helps, principles of interpretation, and a glossary of 100 music terms and expressions are some of the many helps available. 48 pp.